SAVING ENDANGERED SPECIES

THE
AMERICAN CROCODILE
Help Save This Endangered Species!

Glenn Scherer and
Marty Fletcher

MyReportLinks.com Books

an imprint of

Enslow Publishers, Inc.   E

Box 398, 40 Industrial Road
Berkeley Heights, NJ 07922
USA

MyReportLinks.com Books, an imprint of Enslow Publishers, Inc. MyReportLinks®
is a registered trademark of Enslow Publishers, Inc.

Library of Congress Cataloging-in-Publication Data

Scherer, Glenn.
   The American crocodile : help save this endangered species! / Glenn Scherer and Marty
Fletcher.
      p. cm. – (Saving endangered species)
   Includes bibliographical references and index.
   ISBN-13: 978-1-59845-041-5
   ISBN-10: 1-59845-041-7
   1. American crocodile—Juvenile literature. I. Fletcher, Marty. II. Title.
QL666.C925S34 2007
597.98'2—dc22
                                        2006023503

Printed in the United States of America

10 9 8 7 6 5 4 3 2 1

To Our Readers:
Through the purchase of this book, you and your library gain access to the Report Links that specifically
back up this book.
The Publisher will provide access to the Report Links that back up this book and will keep these Report
Links up to date on **www.myreportlinks.com** for five years from the book's first publication date.
We have done our best to make sure all Internet addresses in this book were active and appropriate when
we went to press. However, the author and the Publisher have no control over, and assume no liability
for, the material available on those Internet sites or on other Web sites they may link to.
The usage of the MyReportLinks.com Books Web site is subject to the terms and conditions stated on the
Usage Policy Statement on **www.myreportlinks.com**.
A password may be required to access the Report Links that back up this book. The password is found
on the bottom of page 4 of this book.
Any comments or suggestions can be sent by e-mail to comments@myreportlinks.com or to the address
on the back cover.

Photo Credits: © Clipart.com, p. 87; © Corel Corporation, pp. 47, 68–69; © Coverstock/
Shutterstock.com, p. 42; © Frank B. Yuwono/Shutterstock.com, pp. 94–95; © Getty Images, pp. 62–63;
© J. Norman Reid/Shutterstock.com, pp. 32–33, 49, 90–91; © Larsek/Shutterstock.com, p. 54; © Lena
Grottling/Shutterstock.com, pp. 52–53; © Painet Stock Photos, p. 1; © Photos.com, p. 37; © Steve
Cukrov/Shutterstock.com, pp. 34, 70–71, 112–113; © Theresa Martinez/Shutterstock.com, pp. 44–45;
American Museum of Natural History, p. 57; Animal Planet, p. 13; ARKive, p. 74; Crocodile Specialist
Group, University of Florida, pp. 38, 76, 96; Endangered Species Handbook, p. 59; Enslow Publishers,
Inc., p. 5; Everglades National Park Photo, pp. 3, 10, 18–19; Florida Museum of Natural History, p. 30;
MyReportLinks.com Books, p. 4; *National Geographic,* pp. 12, 40, 110; National Park Service, pp. 28, 65,
80; National Wildlife Federation, p. 83; PBS, p. 85; Photograph courtesy University of Florida/IFAS,
p. 16; Project Exploration, p. 25; San Diego National History Museum, p. 22; San Diego Zoo, p. 108; The
Tortoise Reserve, p. 99; The Wildlife Conservation Society, p. 93; U.S. Fish and Wildlife Service, pp. 15,
60, 78, 117; U.S. Geological Survey, p. 115; U.S. House of Representatives, p. 104; University of Florida,
p. 101; University of Georgia, p. 103; University of Michigan, p. 107; Vancouver Aquarium, p. 27.

Cover Photo: © Painet Stock Photos.

CONTENTS

MyReportLinks.com Books
Great Books, Great Links, Great for Research!

The Internet sites featured in this book can save you hours of research time. These Internet sites—we call them **"Report Links"**—are constantly changing, but we keep them up to date on our Web site.

When you see this "Approved Web Site" logo, you will know that we are directing you to a great Internet site that will help you with your research.

Give it a try! Type http://www.myreportlinks.com into your browser, click on the series title and enter the password, then click on the book title, and scroll down to the Report Links listed for this book.

The Report Links will bring you to great source documents, photographs, and illustrations. MyReportLinks.com Books save you time, feature Report Links that are kept up to date, and make report writing easier than ever! A complete listing of the Report Links can be found on pages 118–119 at the back of the book.

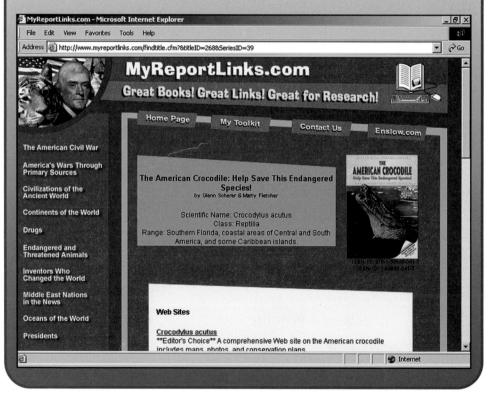

Please see "To Our Readers" on the copyright page for important information about this book, the MyReportLinks.com Web site, and the Report Links that back up this book.

Please enter **ACS1773** if asked for a password.

AMERICAN CROCODILE FACTS

▶ **Scientific Name**
Crocodylus acutus

▶ **Earliest Crocodilian Ancestors Evolved**
200 million years ago

▶ **Maximum Length**
15 feet (4.6 meters) in Florida. Outside Florida, in warmer habitats that better support the American crocodile, individuals have been known to grow to as large as 23 feet (7 meters).

▶ **Weight**
Males weigh from about 500 to 1,000 pounds (220 to 450 kilograms).

▶ **Top Leaping Distance**
Even large crocodilians are able to vault nearly vertically out of the water to a height of more than 5 feet (1.5 meters) to snap at birds or other animals.

▶ **Range**
The American crocodile is found in North, Central, and South America, specifically on Caribbean islands, in areas that border the Caribbean Sea, and on the Pacific Ocean coast of Central America. The countries where it is known to be found are Belize, Colombia, Costa Rica, Cuba, the Dominican Republic, Ecuador, El Salvador, Guatemala, Haiti, Honduras, Jamaica, Mexico, Nicaragua, Panama, Peru, the United States (Florida), and Venezuela.

▶ **Habitat**
The American crocodile is found primarily in mangrove-lined ocean bays and sounds, in brackish river mouths and tidal creeks, and in inland swamps. It lives in both saltwater and freshwater.

▶ **Diet**
Adult American crocodiles are carnivores and feed mostly on fish, but also on crabs, snakes, frogs, turtles, small and large birds, small mammals, and aquatic invertebrates. They will eat carrion (the flesh of dead or dying animals) and will cannibalize baby crocodiles. Hatchling crocodiles survive mostly on insects while juveniles will consume tadpoles, frogs, snails, crabs, shrimp, and small fish.

▶ Sexual Maturity

Female American crocodiles reach sexual maturity when they are about 7.4 feet (2.25 meters) in length, a size they reach usually between the ages of 10 and 13 years.

▶ When Eggs Are Laid

April to May in Florida, Mexico, Venezuela, and Honduras; December to February in Ecuador and Panama; mid-February to early April in the Dominican Republic; and late March to early May in Belize.

▶ Number of Eggs in a Clutch

Females deposit elongated oval eggs into their nests, but the number of eggs, or clutch size, depends upon the habitat. Clutch sizes can range from as low as eight eggs to as high as fifty-six eggs. In Florida, the average is thirty-eight.

▶ Incubation Period

About eighty-six days

▶ Life Span

Fifty to seventy years

▶ Date Protected

The American crocodile was listed under the U.S. Endangered Species Act on September 25, 1975. The American crocodile was listed as a United Nations Convention on International Trade in Endangered Species of Wild Fauna and Flora (CITES) Appendix I species (given full protection from international commerce), on June 6, 1981.

▶ Population

The total number of American crocodiles in the world today is estimated at around 10,000 to 20,000, with as many as 1,200 of them found in Florida.

▶ Major Threats

Current threats include hunting, poaching, and killing as pests outside Florida. Habitat loss, habitat fragmentation, and habitat degradation are major problems throughout the American crocodile's range. In the future, climate change could become a major threat.

It is a mystery to me why people act with fear, or want to make friends, with crocodiles, neither of which is the appropriate response. We should look at them with a mixture of awe and respect, not fear and revulsion.

—*Dr. Frank J. Mazzotti*

Chapter 1 ▶

MEETING WITH A CROCODILE

When most people think of crocodiles, they probably imagine man-eating monsters from fairy tales, like the ferocious "croc" that swallowed up Captain Hook in *Peter Pan*. But Dr. Frank Mazzotti, a wildlife ecologist with the University of Florida, thinks of one crocodile species quite differently. "My experience with the American crocodile? I tend to characterize it as the sweetheart of the crocodilian world. It is one of the least aggressive of any of the crocodilian species and certainly the least aggressive among large crocodiles."[1]

Mazzotti tells a fascinating story to prove his point. In the 1970s, he was in Everglades National Park doing research on the American crocodile, trying to save the last surviving members of this endangered species living in southern Florida. "What we did when the eggs hatched is to routinely conduct population surveys both day and night. In the daytime we were looking for nests that hatch. At nighttime we were looking for the babies themselves," he said. "Everything we do [as scientists] begins with marking hatchling

▲ *An American crocodile in Everglades National Park. One way to identify the reptile is by observing its mouth when fully closed. The fourth and largest lower tooth fits into a socket in its upper jaw and is always visible, which makes the crocodile appear to be grinning.*

crocodiles. Once the animals are marked, we can follow them as they grow, nest, and survive, which is a very important part of our job."[2]

On one particularly sultry, mosquito-infested, tropical night, Mazzotti was joined by a coworker as they searched for American crocodiles along the South Florida coast. He described their outing:

"We did like we always do: took out a boat and patrolled the shoreline at a very high rate of speed, shining a light. And when the light hit the eyes of those critters, it reflected back at us like bicycle reflectors. Even the baby crocodiles are quite easy to pick out this way at night."[3]

When Mazzotti spotted some shining eyes ashore, he stopped the boat, landed, and tried to catch the newly hatched crocodiles. "In this case, when I found the babies, I also found mom," Mazzotti recalls. "Mom" was a large full-grown crocodile. "I walked right up to mom and the kids, and with a set of tongs scooped up a whole bunch of the babies, right off the mother's snout. She didn't act upset. She just sat there and let us go about our business. I was a little surprised when I got that close that the animal didn't retreat. I would pick up one baby, put it in the bag, pick up another baby, put it in a bag, and mom didn't make a move. She was neither afraid, nor did she come after us. That was a really very dramatic experience."[4]

Mazzotti and his fellow team member marked the crocodiles, weighed and measured them, and then released them, in the hopes they would spot them again soon and be able to track their growth.

"I mark them by clipping their tail scutes [bony plates], according to a prescribed sequence to give them a unique code, removing little pieces of their

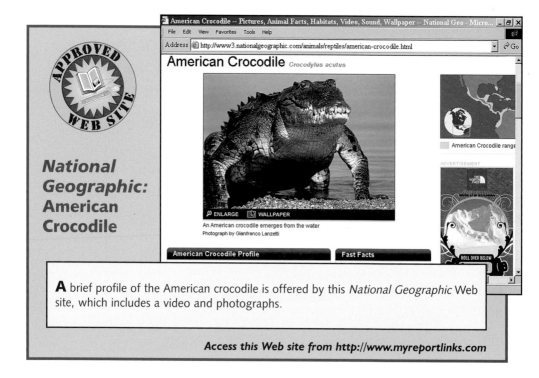

American Crocodile -- Pictures, Animal Facts, Habitats, Video, Sound, Wallpaper -- National Geo - Micro...

File   Edit   View   Favorites   Tools   Help

Address   http://www3.nationalgeographic.com/animals/reptiles/american-crocodile.html

American Crocodile *Crocodylus acutus*

American Crocodile range

ADVERTISEMENT

ENLARGE   WALLPAPER

An American crocodile emerges from the water
Photograph by Gianfranco Lanzetti

American Crocodile Profile   Fast Facts   ROLL OVER BELOW

National Geographic: American Crocodile

A brief profile of the American crocodile is offered by this *National Geographic* Web site, which includes a video and photographs.

Access this Web site from http://www.myreportlinks.com

skin. So far, our record interval is eighteen years between capturing an animal as a hatchling and recapturing it as an adult."[5]

To emphasize just how gentle and nonaggressive American crocodiles can be, Mazzotti makes a comparison: "Think about this for a second. You are walking down the street one night, minding your own business, and this van pulls up next to you, and the door swings open, and this bright light hits you in the eyes and blinds you. The next thing you know, this wire snare goes around your neck, and it jerks tighter twice. Then total strangers haul you into the van, they blindfold you, they weigh and measure you. Now I bet by this time you wouldn't be in a particularly good humor! Well, we do this to American crocodiles routinely, and they just lay there. You'll find other species of crocodilians that are far more aggressive. American alligators, for example, will put up a tussle for a half hour or more before they'll let you subdue them. American crocodiles cooperate. I've never been bitten while capturing an animal. You don't get bit. It's not like on TV."[6]

Mazzotti described his frustration with the way crocodiles are commonly perceived: "It is a mystery to me why people act with fear, or want to make friends, with crocodiles, neither of which is the appropriate response," he says. "We should

This Animal Planet site offers photographs of all twenty-three species of crocodilians. Unlike some other species, American crocodiles are far from ferocious—except to their prey.

Access this Web site from http://www.myreportlinks.com

look at them with a mixture of awe and respect, not fear and revulsion. If there is one thing I could tell kids, that would be it. That is like all of nature. Nature is not something to be feared but to be respected. And the more you learn about it, the more you love it."[7]

A Strange and Ancient Beast

Crocodilians, which include all of the world's species of crocodiles, alligators, and the gharial of India, are remarkably ancient animals. They have existed since the age of the dinosaurs, with an evolutionary line stretching back more than 200 million years. The earliest crocodilians not only lived among the dinosaurs, but they also fed on small ones.

The American crocodile (*Crocodylus acutus*) is one of the largest and least aggressive crocodilians. It lives in the southernmost part of Florida, including the Florida Keys; on some islands in the Caribbean Sea; and along the Caribbean and Pacific coasts of Central and South America.

The American crocodile is an animal under siege from human pressures in all of its range. In some places, it has been hunted nearly to extinction for its meat and for its hide, which has been used to make luggage, handbags, belts, boots, shoes, and other articles of clothing. Damage to and loss of habitat is also a threat to the American crocodile. In southern Florida, development had greatly endangered this species by the 1970s.

The Good News in Florida

Thanks to policies put into practice under the Endangered Species Act, the American crocodile is recovering well in Florida, with a population of about one thousand. Recently, the United States Fish and Wildlife Service (USFWS or FWS) began to consider down-listing the American crocodile in Florida as a threatened species. It would still receive federal protection, but would not be classified as currently facing extinction. Officials with FWS point out that since the crocodile's population has more than doubled since 1975, when it

ENDANGERED SPECIES PROGRAM KID'S CORNER - Microsoft Internet Explorer

File   Edit   View   Favorites   Tools   Help

Address http://www.fws.gov/endangered/kids/index.html   Go

U.S. Fish & Wildlife Service

Kid's Corner

Endangered Means There Is Still Time
Species Spotlight | How Can Kids Help? | Educators
Learn More | Endangered Species Program

Endangered Means There is Still Time

USFWS Endangered Species Program Kid's Corner

On this page, the United States Fish and Wildlife Service (USFWS), which is responsible for protecting endangered species, offers ways in which you can become involved in saving those species and our environment.

Access this Web site from http://www.myreportlinks.com

▲ "Croc Doc" Dr. Frank Mazzotti of the University of Florida, a wildlife ecologist, has been at the forefront of the effort to survey South Florida's American crocodile population and help preserve it.

was listed as endangered, its status should be changed.[8] A change in listing status will not happen right away, but the very fact that it is being considered is a sign that efforts to save the American crocodile in Florida have made a difference. Those efforts must continue if the species is to survive.

▷ Why Save the American Crocodile?

People have loathed crocodiles and the mangrove swamps in which they live for thousands of years. That is why many crocodilians have been hunted nearly to extinction, and the wetlands in which they live have been drained.

But Frank Mazzotti argues fiercely for the preservation of the American crocodile. "Why should we be interested in the American crocodile? There are three good reasons," he says. "The first reason to save them is out of scientific curiosity: the fact that these animals are the last of the dinosaurs. Crocodilians are actually archosaurs, the stem group that gave rise to the dinosaurs, the ruling reptiles. Crocodiles provide us with our only chance in today's modern age to get a glimmer of an idea of how the dinosaurs that once ruled the earth survived. To me, that is a pretty darn good reason to want to study them."[9]

Secondly, says Mazzotti, crocodilians are ecologically important. "All crocodilians are top

Protecting critical habitat is essential to saving an endangered species. Since 1975, when the American crocodile was placed on the Endangered Species List, 87 percent of the habitat for this species has been protected in Florida, contributing to its successful recovery there.

predators. Crocodilians are ecosystem engineers upon which other species depend for their existence. They are also indicators of ecosystem health. In the case of the American crocodile, its survival and growth are very strongly related to the flow of freshwater to the South Florida estuary [a body of coastal water where seawater and freshwater mix]. That flow is one of the things we are trying to restore in the Everglades. So, crocodile health is a good way to measure our success in the $8 billion Everglades ecosystem restoration project."[10]

Thirdly, according to Mazzotti, crocodilians can be economically important. In South Florida, the American crocodile has become a species that tourists will pay to see in its natural state. Such tourism is known as ecotourism. "Crocodilians are a destination species. That is, people will spend money to travel to look at them," says Mazzotti. "Whether they are the last of the dinosaurs, whether they are ecologically or economically important, all of those are really good reasons why we should study and preserve crocodiles."[11]

▶ The Future of the American Crocodile

There is a fourth good reason to study the American crocodile. It stands out as one of the few remarkable success stories in the recovery of an endangered species in the United States.

"There is a very positive prognosis for the American crocodile," says Mazzotti, referring to its increase in population since it was first listed as endangered.[12] According to Mazzotti, this success has come about because a substantial amount of the species' habitat has been saved. "We were able to protect most of the critical habitat for the American crocodile, around 87 percent of its existing habitat. That's why crocodiles are thriving in Florida. Protecting that much habitat is absolutely key for [an endangered species'] survival," Mazzotti concludes. "This preservation effort was an absolute success, and it happened only because the American crocodile was declared an endangered species. It is one of the best current arguments against those who are attacking the Endangered Species Act and claiming the law doesn't work. It worked here. It worked in Florida. It worked for the American crocodile."[13]

ALL ABOUT THE AMERICAN CROCODILE

The American crocodile is one of the world's twenty-three species of crocodilians. Crocodilians are the most advanced and largest of the world's living reptiles—cold-blooded animals with backbones that lay eggs and breathe with lungs.

All crocodilian species are adapted to living in warm, mostly tropical and subtropical conditions, always where the land meets the water.

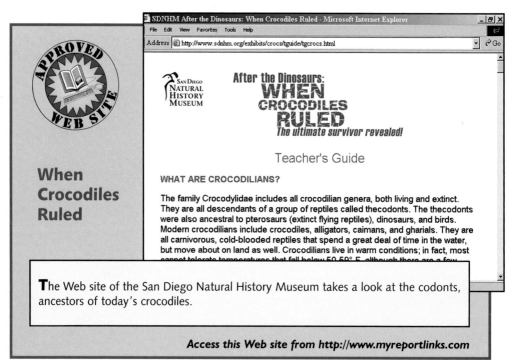

When Crocodiles Ruled

SDNHM After the Dinosaurs: When Crocodiles Ruled - Microsoft Internet Explorer

File   Edit   View   Favorites   Tools   Help

Address http://www.sdnhm.org/exhibits/crocs/tguide/tgcrocs.html

SAN DIEGO NATURAL HISTORY MUSEUM

After the Dinosaurs: WHEN CROCODILES RULED
The ultimate survivor revealed!

Teacher's Guide

WHAT ARE CROCODILIANS?

The family Crocodylidae includes all crocodilian genera, both living and extinct. They are all descendants of a group of reptiles called thecodonts. The thecodonts were also ancestral to pterosaurs (extinct flying reptiles), dinosaurs, and birds. Modern crocodilians include crocodiles, alligators, caimans, and gharials. They are all carnivorous, cold-blooded reptiles that spend a great deal of time in the water, but move about on land as well. Crocodilians live in warm conditions; in fact, most cannot tolerate temperatures that fall below 50-50° F, although there are a few

The Web site of the San Diego Natural History Museum takes a look at the codonts, ancestors of today's crocodiles.

Access this Web site from http://www.myreportlinks.com

Crocodilians especially like mangrove swamps and other marshy and steamy wetlands.

The twenty-three species of crocodilians are divided into three families: Alligator, Gavial, and Crocodile. There are two alligator and six caiman species in the family Alligatoridae; just one species, the true gharial, in the family Gavialidae; and fourteen crocodile species in the family Crocodylidae. Four of these crocodile species live in the American tropics and subtropics. The American crocodile is most widespread throughout that region.

The Evolution of the American Crocodile

As hard as it may be to believe, today's crocodilians are most closely related through evolution not to reptiles but to birds. Like birds, crocodilians sometimes build nests out of plant matter, lay eggs, and take care of their young to some extent. Birds and crocodilians even resemble each other in their biology. "Crocodilians and birds both have an elongate outer-ear canal, a muscular gizzard, and complete separation of the ventricles in the heart," writes author Charles Ross.[1] The reason for the family resemblance between crocodiles and birds is simple: Both may be the last living descendants of the archosaurs, an ancient group of animals that gave rise to the dinosaurs, the flying pterosaurs, the crocodiles, and the birds.

Ancestors of today's crocodilians thrived during the age of the dinosaurs. The most ancient crocodile-like fossils we know of date from about 230 million years ago. These fossils were found in Europe, South America, and South Africa. The oldest true crocodilians date to about 200 million years ago and probably lived only on land. It was later that crocodilians began to live in water also.

▶ Early Crocs

There were many early crocodilians. One of the most spectacular was *Deinosuchus,* or "terror crocodile," which lived in the Cretaceous Period. This gigantic North American predator measured 36 feet (11 meters) in length and weighed up to 6 tons (5.4 metric tons). *Deinosuchus* bones are always found with dinosaur bones, especially those of the plant-eating duck-billed dinosaurs called hadrosaurs. Some paleontologists, there-fore, think that *Deinosuchus,* rather than the big meat-eating tyrannosaurs, may have been the main predator of the hadrosaurs. A reconstructed *Deinosuchus* skull is huge when compared with the skulls of today's largest crocodilians. A grown man could easily fit inside its immense jaws.

Crocodilians seem to have been nearly unaf-fected by the great extinction that killed the dinosaurs 65 million years ago. To this day, pale-ontologists do not know why these animals

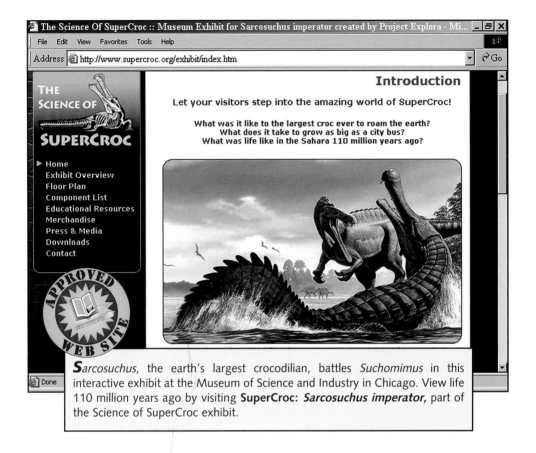

The Science Of SuperCroc :: Museum Exhibit for Sarcosuchus imperator created by Project Explora - Mi...

File   Edit   View   Favorites   Tools   Help

Address http://www.supercroc.org/exhibit/index.htm

THE SCIENCE OF SUPERCROC

▶ Home
Exhibit Overview
Floor Plan
Component List
Educational Resources
Merchandise
Press & Media
Downloads
Contact

APPROVED WEB SITE

Introduction

Let your visitors step into the amazing world of SuperCroc!

What was it like to the largest croc ever to roam the earth?
What does it take to grow as big as a city bus?
What was life like in the Sahara 110 million years ago?

Done

Sarcosuchus, the earth's largest crocodilian, battles *Suchomimus* in this interactive exhibit at the Museum of Science and Industry in Chicago. View life 110 million years ago by visiting **SuperCroc: *Sarcosuchus imperator*,** part of the Science of SuperCroc exhibit.

survived. It is one of the fascinating mysteries about crocodilians that may be solved by our next generation of scientists.

Very little is known about the evolution of the modern American crocodile since the extinction of dinosaurs, because little fossil evidence has been found or examined. It is known that as the earth cooled during the ice ages of the last 3 million years, most crocodilians, including the American crocodile, retreated to the subtropics and tropics. That is where they remain today.

The evolutionary design of the crocodile has withstood the test of time. It is so well adapted that most of its features have changed only slightly over the past 200 million years. Survivors for all that time, crocodilians have only really become threatened since the arrival of modern human beings. Though many crocodilian species were able to survive whatever event doomed the dinosaurs, and those same species have survived the relentless cold of ice ages, many of them might not last through this century. The effects of humans, including hunting, habitat loss, and habitat degradation, may yet doom them.

What Is in a Name?

The name *crocodile* first came into use to describe these large reptiles about two thousand years ago when the ancient Greeks traveled to Egypt. There, on the Nile River, they saw large animals that they thought resembled a little lizard they knew from back home. They called this lizard *krokodeilos,* which means "pebble worm."

The American crocodile's scientific name is *Crocodylus acutus* (*acutus* is Latin for "sharp" or "pointed"), which refers to the animal's elongated snout. But it goes by many other names in the other parts of its range: Cocodrilo americano, Crocodile d'Amérique, Caimán de Aguja, Central American alligator, Cocodrilo de Rio, Crocodile à

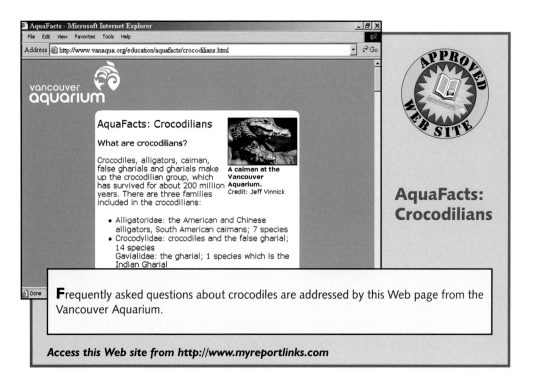

AquaFacts: Crocodilians

What are crocodilians?

Crocodiles, alligators, caiman, false gharials and gharials make up the crocodilian group, which has survived for about 200 million years. There are three families included in the crocodilians:

A caiman at the Vancouver Aquarium.
Credit: Jeff Vinnick

- Alligatoridae: the American and Chinese alligators, South American caimans; 7 species
- Crocodylidae: crocodiles and the false gharial; 14 species
  Gavialidae: the gharial; 1 species which is the Indian Gharial

AquaFacts: Crocodilians

Frequently asked questions about crocodiles are addressed by this Web page from the Vancouver Aquarium.

Access this Web site from http://www.myreportlinks.com

museau pointu, Lagarto Amarillo, Lagarto Real, Llaman Caimán, South American alligator, and American saltwater crocodile.[2]

▶ Comparing Crocodiles, Alligators, and Gharials

To most people, alligators and crocodiles look pretty much alike. But with a little training and close observation, you can learn to recognize them in pictures, if not in person.

The best way to tell a crocodile from an alligator or a gharial is to look at its snout. A gharial has long, thin jaws with a knob at the end, which makes its snout look something like a baseball bat.

Alligators have wide, flat heads with blunt, rounded noses. Crocodiles have much more narrow, triangular-shaped pointed heads.

In Florida, you can also tell the difference between an American alligator and an American crocodile by how they bask, or warm themselves at rest. The crocodile generally basks with its mouth open and teeth showing, to better regulate its temperature. The alligator basks with its mouth fully closed.

If both the alligator and the crocodile have their mouths closed, you can still tell them apart. If you look closely, you will see that the largest lower tooth of the American crocodile fits into a

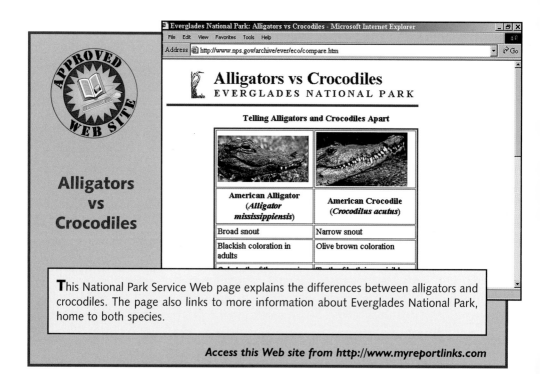

This National Park Service Web page explains the differences between alligators and crocodiles. The page also links to more information about Everglades National Park, home to both species.

Access this Web site from http://www.myreportlinks.com

notch in its upper jaw and is fully visible when its mouth is closed. The alligator's biggest teeth are hidden in its mouth when its mouth is closed. "If the animal looks as if it is leering at you when its jaws are closed, it's a crocodile," write John and Deborah Behler in their book *Alligators and Crocodiles*.[3]

You can also tell the difference by color. American alligators appear black when wet and dark gray when dry. Juvenile American crocodiles are light in color, yellowish tan to gray with dark cross-markings on the body and tail. In older animals, these markings fade, and the body turns an olive-brown or tan.

You can also tell the difference between these reptile species by where you find them: American crocodiles generally inhabit saltwater or brackish water, while American alligators prefer freshwater. The reason for this has to do with a body part that the species have in common but that functions differently in each. Both crocodiles and alligators have special glands in their tongues that allow them to get rid of too much salt, but the alligator's glands do not work as well as the crocodile's.

A Large Animal

The American crocodile can reach an average of 20 feet (6 meters) in length, though it does not grow this large throughout its entire range. In

Crocodilian Species - American Crocodile (Crocodylus acutus) - Microsoft Internet Explorer

File   Edit   View   Favorites   Tools   Help

Address http://www.flmnh.ufl.edu/alligatorfund/lcacu1.htm

« main
« maps
« heads

FAMILY:
ALLIGATORIDAE

A. mississippiensis
A. sinensis
C. crocodilus
C. c. apaporiensis
C. c. fuscus
C. latirostris
C. yacare
M. niger
P. palpebrosus
P. trig

C. ini
C. johns
C. mind
C. mora

Crocodylus acutus

An adult American crocodile, as seen from the front, displaying its relatively narrow and pointed snout. Crocodiles from further south in the species' distribution tends to have an even narrower snout (perhaps to enable a different prey niche to be exploited next to the broader-snouted caimans with which it shares its range). This animal was photographed in Florida, at the northernmost limit of its distribution. It is just possible to make out the bony median ridge which runs approximately halfway down the animal's upper jaw from the back of the head.

Photograph © Adam Britton

ALL IMAGES:

The Florida Museum of Natural History has devoted a site to each of the twenty-three species of crocodilians. On this page from the *Crocodylus acutus* site, learn about what distinguishes the American crocodile from other crocodilians.

EDITOR'S CHOICE

Florida, for example, the animals are living at the northernmost part of their range, where they rarely grow bigger than 15 feet (4.6 meters). Outside Florida, in warmer habitats that better support the American crocodile, individuals have been known to grow as large as 23 feet (7 meters).

Males are usually larger than females, weighing an average of 500 to 1,000 pounds (220 to 450 kilograms), but they can weigh as much as 2,000 pounds (907 kilograms). As with most crocodilians, 80 percent of their body weight is in muscle and armored skin.

A Fierce Predator

Crocodilians in most parts of the world are top predators, meaning that they are at the top of the food chain. Few other animals will challenge them. The American crocodile is no exception. Adult American crocodiles feed mostly on fish, but they also eat crabs, snakes, frogs, turtles, small and large birds, and small mammals. They have been known to eat carrion and will cannibalize baby crocodiles. Hatchling crocodiles survive mostly on insects, while juveniles will eat tadpoles, frogs, snails, crabs, shrimp, and small fish.

Once an American crocodile catches any of these creatures between its strong jaws and drags it beneath the water, there is little the prey can do to survive. The crocodile's teeth and jaw are perfectly adapted for puncturing, gripping, and crushing its prey.

The American crocodile is especially good at stalking its prey. It can lie still in the water, camouflaged like a mud-splattered floating log, with its eyes, ears, and nostrils just peaking above the surface. To some, it resembles the conning tower of a submarine. When a small mammal or another animal approaches, the crocodile suddenly lashes into action, catching and consuming its prey in

Even though the American crocodile has sharp teeth and a strong jaw ideal for catching prey, it is unable to chew that prey because of its long, flat mouth and lack of lips. Instead, it mauls what it catches before swallowing it whole.

seconds. It will also vomit up bits of its food to lure fish closer.

The American crocodile, like other crocodilians, is unable to chew its food, so it mauls its prey, then swallows it whole. Its stomach is especially adapted to handle this "whole food." Its digestive system is the most acidic known of any vertebrate, allowing it to digest all the bone that it consumes.

▲ *The eyes, nostrils, and ears of an American crocodile are situated on top of its head so that the rest of its body can remain motionless under water while it hunts for prey. An idle crocodile can hold its breath for up to two hours.*

American crocodiles are nocturnal, typically active from just before sunset to shortly after sunrise. They spend most of this time foraging for food. Like other crocodilians, the American crocodile spends most of its hunting time lying in wait of its prey. It stays camouflaged in mud and algae. Then it strikes with amazing speed across the water or up onto a nearby beach. Even large crocodilians can jump more than 5 feet (1.5 meters) from the water to snap at birds or other prey.[4]

Crocodilians do not have to eat constantly, however. Their tails can store a tremendous amount of food as fat. Even a hatchling crocodilian can live for more than four months without eating. A large crocodile can, if it has to, go for two years without a meal.

Getting Around on Land and in Water

The American crocodile is ideally suited for life both on land and in the water. It has four short, thick legs that allow it to move quickly over land, but it also has a powerful tail. That tail, which is longer than the rest of its body, whips back and forth when the crocodile swims.

The crocodile's broad and stubby front feet have five toes each for firm footing on land. Each back foot has only four toes, but they are long ones, helping the animal to walk and also steer in water, like rudders. The crocodile's body is sleek and long, making it a graceful swimmer. Though it is more awkward on land, it can still achieve short bursts of speed there.

The American crocodile, like other crocodilians, has two primary ways of walking on land. When moving slowly, it can crawl with its belly close to the ground and its legs splayed out. When it needs to move faster, as when it is chasing down prey, it can go into a high walk: Its belly is carried high off the ground, while fully extended limbs project from under the body. Crocodiles can even go into a "gallop" for short distances, which makes them fierce and dangerous hunters.

Vocal Reptiles: Crocodile Communication

Author Charles A. Ross calls crocodiles "the loud-mouths of the reptile world."[5] They make a wide variety of vocalizations, ranging from what Ross describes as "barely audible coughs and hisses, to high volume roars and bellows."[6]

At times—during mating or when establishing territories, for example—crocodiles can be very social animals. At such times, they have many ways of communicating with other members of their species. The American crocodile can convey messages through sounds, postures, motions, odors, and touch.

Crocodile communication actually begins while the animal is still in the egg, a characteristic

▲ *American crocodiles are territorial creatures, particularly the males when vying for mates. While direct combat and injury are rare, adult male crocs show aggression by opening their jaws when challengers are near.*

also found in bird species. Some people doubt this ability to "talk" while still in the egg, but the following description of a laboratory experiment with American crocodiles seems to show that such communication can happen:

> Eggs . . . responded to sounds made near the eggs as well as to sounds coming from within nearby eggs, during the final two weeks of incubation. Tapping lightly on the container resulted in "pecking" sounds from within individual eggs. Later, a microphone buried with the eggs revealed that tapping sounds from inside one egg were answered within seconds by similar sounds from adjacent eggs.[7]

Some scientists think that such communication from inside the egg can help to synchronize hatching, which always happens on one night and at roughly the same moment for all the eggs in a clutch.

Once hatched, baby American crocodiles spontaneously begin communicating using distinctive calls, yelps, and grunts. Each call is thought to have a particular meaning. A person picking up a hatchling, for example, will hear it give a "distress" call to which either or both of the adult crocodiles will respond. In fact, some poachers

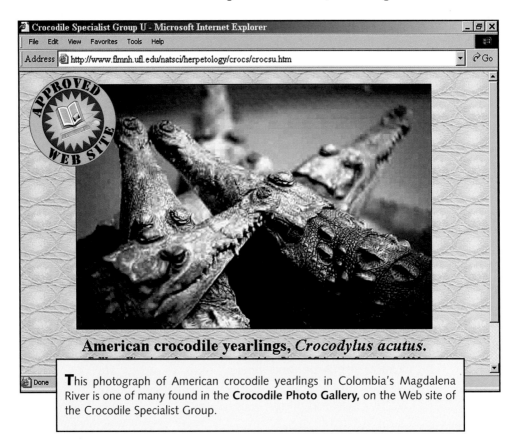

American crocodile yearlings, *Crocodylus acutus.*

This photograph of American crocodile yearlings in Colombia's Magdalena River is one of many found in the **Crocodile Photo Gallery,** on the Web site of the Crocodile Specialist Group.

actually imitate this hatchling distress call in order to lure parent crocodiles to their deaths.

Crocodiles also communicate with each other by using other loud sounds such as a head slap or jaw clap in the water, both good at getting attention. Dominant male American crocodiles may head slap two or three times quickly from their own territories.[8] Head slapping, says author Ross, is associated with establishing and maintaining long-term social relationships. Surprisingly, a loud noise, such as a vehicle backfiring or a gun going off, can sometimes make crocodiles slap heads.

The American crocodile also communicates during courtship through vibrations or low-frequency signals known as infrasound, sounds too low to be heard by the human ear. Infrasound is created by contracting the body muscles just beneath the surface of the water, resulting in tiny radiating pulses of waves. If people could hear such sounds, they would sound like faraway thunder.

▶ The American Crocodile's Range

The American crocodile lives in seventeen North, Central, and South American countries: Belize, Colombia, Costa Rica, Cuba, the Dominican Republic, Ecuador, El Salvador, Guatemala, Haiti, Honduras, Jamaica, Mexico, Nicaragua, Panama,

Peru, the United States, and Venezuela. The animal may also inhabit the islands of Martinique and Trinidad and Tobogo.

The American crocodile reaches the extreme northern edge of its range in southernmost Florida and on Mexico's Yucatán Peninsula. It lives as far south as Ecuador, Colombia, Venezuela, and Peru in South America.

In Florida, the American crocodile's historical range was as far north on the East Coast as Lake Worth, Palm Beach County, and as far north as Tampa Bay on the Gulf Coast. It ranged as far south as Key West. Today its range has shrunk to include only coastal areas of Miami-Dade,

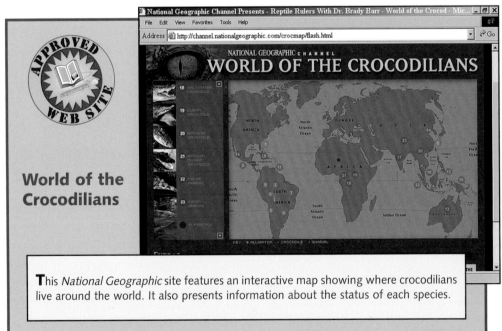

World of the Crocodilians

This *National Geographic* site features an interactive map showing where crocodilians live around the world. It also presents information about the status of each species.

Access this Web site from http://www.myreportlinks.com

Monroe, Collier, and Lee counties. Crocodiles are regularly seen in Everglades National Park, along the mainland shoreline of Florida Bay and Biscayne Bay. A few have recently been seen as far south as Key West, which leads some biologists to wonder if this endangered species is again expanding its range in Florida.

A Heat-Loving Animal

There is a very good reason why the American crocodile is sandwiched into the tropical and subtropical zones and unable to live in cooler more temperate zones. Like most other crocodilians, it is poikilothermic. Like snakes, lizards and turtles, the American crocodile's internal body temperature depends on the outside air and water temperature. It lacks insulation such as feathers or hair, which could warm or cool the body, and it cannot shiver to get warm. So almost all crocodilians, including the American crocodile, live in parts of the world that have an average temperature warmer than 50 to 59°F (10 to 15°C).

The American crocodile shares its range with several other crocodilians. It shares southern Florida with the American alligator *(Alligator mississippiensis)*, Mexico and parts of Central America with Morelet's crocodile *(Crocodylus moreletii)* and the common caiman *(Caiman*

▲ Mangrove swamps are vital to the health of coastal ecosystems, providing refuge, nesting grounds (here, for an osprey pair), and food to a vast number of land and water species. They also act as a buffer zone against storms so that land erosion and property damage are lessened or avoided altogether.

crocodilus), and Cuba with the Cuban crocodile (*Crocodylus rhombifer*). The American crocodile prefers more salty waters than any of these other species, though they may share similar habitats. In Florida, the American crocodile and American alligator have probably peacefully coexisted for thousands of years. The amount of salinity, or salt, in the water determines which animal is more numerous in each area. The two species rarely nest side by side, although this has been known to happen.

▶ The Mangrove Habitat

The American crocodile lives primarily in mangrove-lined ocean bays and sounds, brackish river mouths and tidal creeks, and inland swamps. A mangrove is a type of tropical evergreen that grows in large communities in salty water. Its dense roots form tangled swampy masses.

In the past, people viewed mangrove swamps as mosquito- and crocodile-infested places that were not worth preserving. Throughout much of the twentieth century, mangroves were cut down to build beach resorts and other developments. In the process, however, the destruction of these rich ecosystems also killed many animal and plant species, and many of those are now endangered. For example, the destruction of the mangrove forests at Isla Fuerte on the coast of Colombia,

It is in and along mangrove channels like these that American crocodiles make their home. Unfortunately, human exploitation of this natural resource without replenishing it has a negative affect on both animals and people. Products such as charcoal, hair oil, incense, honey, and construction materials are all made from mangrove trees.

South America, resulted in the extinction of American crocodiles there.[9]

Thankfully, our thinking about mangrove forests has changed. We now know that mangroves support tremendous biodiversity and provide nurseries for many commercially and recreationally valuable fish and shellfish. Scientists estimate that as much as 75 percent of all fish commercially caught either spend some time in mangrove habitats or depend on food chains that include these coastal forests.[10]

Mangroves may also offer protection against tsunamis. Had the mangrove swamps of coastal Asia been left in place, it is possible that not as many lives would have been lost in the great tsunami that brought such destruction to Indonesia, Thailand, and India in December 2004. To protect the American crocodile, we must also protect mangroves. By doing that, we are also protecting our commercial fisheries and human communities from storm damage.

Other Homes for Crocodiles

American crocodiles also live in several freshwater habitats located well inland, including a number of reservoirs. One of the largest populations of American crocodiles is in a lake: Lago Enriquillo, in the Dominican Republic, a landlocked salt lake that lies below sea level.[11]

American crocodiles have also found a home for themselves in the artificial canals used for nuclear power plants. The use of these artificial canals has helped to replace natural habitat lost to the animals.

Finding Mates and Having Babies

Female American crocodiles reach sexual maturity between the ages of 10 and 13. At that point, they have grown to about 7.4 feet (2.25 meters) in length. As with most crocodilians, courtship and

▲ *While earth has undergone many changes throughout the American crocodile's 200-million-year existence, the species has changed very little. The American crocodile still looks a lot like its crocodilian ancestors of millions of years ago.*

mating occur when the American crocodile is stimulated by rising temperatures in both the air and water. In South Florida, temperatures high enough to trigger courtship behavior are reached by late February through March. This timing, however, varies throughout the rest of the crocodile's range. Once it is reached, the complex courtship rituals can last for two months.

Breeding is polygynous, meaning that each breeding male may mate with several females. Males defend their territories and the females they mate with by loud vocalizations, body posturing, and aggressive behavior.

Nesting Behaviors

The female American crocodile builds her nest by digging out a hole in a sandy beach, riverbank, or canal bank next to relatively deep water. Where these materials are not available, the crocodile digs a hole in vegetation, lays her eggs, and then piles more plant debris on top of the nest. She may dig several trial, or false, nests near the true nest. There are nesting variations throughout the American crocodile's range, however. In Florida, more than one female may use the same nest in different years. But in Mexico, nesting females are more territorial. Elsewhere, especially in the Caribbean, communal nesting is common.

The success of nesting depends on the nest and eggs staying moist enough throughout incubation.

▲ *An American crocodile in Everglades National Park. Even in protected areas, crocodile eggs are destroyed by predators.*

Drought, flooding, and predation by animals like raccoons can destroy nests. On the South Florida mainland, about 13 percent of nests monitored are affected by flooding or drying out. Another 13 percent are partially or entirely destroyed by egg-eating predators.

Clutch sizes vary depending on habitat. They range from as low as eight to as high as fifty-six eggs. The clutch takes about eighty-six days to incubate and hatch. During that time, the female regularly visits the nest. Some females outside the United States have been known to stay with their nests or even defend them against humans, though this behavior has not been seen in Florida. All breeding females must return to their nests to help dig the young nestlings out.

Difficult Beginnings

Hatchlings measure approximately 10.6 inches (27 centimeters) in length. They stay together for several days or weeks following hatching but are rarely seen with their parents. Hatchlings find shelter during the day in the tangles of mangrove roots or beach debris. Because so many predators feed on the baby crocs, their survival rate is usually quite low but can vary depending on location. In Everglades National Park, for example, less than 5 percent of hatchlings survive to adulthood. In northern Key Largo's more sheltered habitats, survival rates have been found to be as high as 20.4 percent. Hatchlings born on unsheltered beaches seem to fare the worst. There, they might be eaten by wading birds, gulls, blue crabs, sharks, and other crocodiles.

Not Commonly a Man-Eater

Unlike the Nile crocodile *(Crocodylus niloticus)* and the Australian saltwater crocodile *(Crocodylus porosus)* who are well-known man-eaters, the American crocodile tends to shy away from people. There has never been a report of an unprovoked attack by an American crocodile on a human in South Florida.

Although these crocodiles are not typically aggressive, the public perception of them is otherwise. Many people living in Florida as well as some of the many tourists who vacation there imagine the American crocodile to be a ferocious killer, lurking in canals and other waterways, just waiting to attack passersby. Urban legends—lies and tall tales—like the following continue to be spread about the species. This appeared anony-mously on the Internet:

> A foursome was playing golf at Palm Beach's ritzi-est country club. One guy lost his ball in a water hazard and started fishing around for it. The other three golfers waited awhile, but finally went ahead with their round. Eventually they started looking for him. Next to the pond they found only his clubs.
>
> The next day somebody spotted the giant American crocodile known as "Old Mose" . . . sunbathing near the eighth tee. He looked plump and well-fed. A state trapper caught him and slit open its stomach [and found the golfer inside].[12]

This legend was accompanied by a gory photo of a crocodile being opened up, with a human body found inside—except that the picture was of a crocodile in Indonesia. While American crocodiles have sometimes wandered onto golf courses, they have never attacked anyone there.

The other reason many people fear American crocodiles is because they confuse them with

An American crocodile in Florida. South Florida is the only place in the world where crocodiles and alligators coexist.

American alligators, which are much greater in number and also more aggressive. There have been twenty fatal American alligator assaults on people since the 1940s. The American crocodile's mistaken reputation as a ferocious killer makes it

▲ *In this photo of an American alligator, notice its U-shaped, rounded snout. A crocodile's snout is generally longer and more V-shaped, but the similarities between alligators and crocodiles often make it difficult to tell one from the other.*

difficult for wildlife officials to get public support to preserve the species. "If you don't solve the problem of human intolerance, your preservation program will never be a success," according to Dr. Frank Mazzotti.[13]

While there have been no reports of American crocodiles attacking humans in Florida, there have been attacks in other places in the species' range. This may have something to do with their size. Florida crocodiles rarely grow over 15 feet (4.6 meters) long, while elsewhere they can grow to more than 20 feet (6.1 meters) in length. This larger size might make them more likely to go after larger prey such as human beings. Still, the records of attacks are not conclusive. The greatest threat to the American crocodile—no matter where it lives or how aggressive it may be—is still the threat posed by human beings.

THREATS TO THE SPECIES

No one really knows just how many American crocodiles once lived throughout their range before European settlers arrived, but scientists believe that by the early twentieth century, there were between 1,000 and 2,000 in the United States. That number was probably reduced by hunting and museum collecting.

By the 1970s, the number of American crocodiles in Florida fell as low as between 100 and 400, mostly due to habitat loss (especially around the growing city of Miami), commercial hunting, killing as pests, and collisions with automobiles.

While the Endangered Species Act has allowed for a dramatic recovery by the American crocodile in Florida, the animal has not done so well in other parts of its range. There, it may not be protected at all, or if it is protected, that protection is not well enforced. Current threats in these regions include continued hunting, poaching, and habitat loss and degradation. In some areas of Central

AMNH - Expedition : Endangered - Microsoft Internet Explorer

File Edit View Favorites Tools Help

Address http://www.amnh.org/nationalcenter/Endangered/croc/croc.html Go

American Crocodile
Crocodylus acutus

APPROVED WEB SITE

Endangered!: American Crocodile

Threats
habitat destruction, illegal hunting for

Old Family . . . New Problems
Crocodiles are often referred to as "living fossils." They have the same basic appearance and lifestyle that they had nearly 200 million years

View the interaction between the American crocodile and its habitat on this American Museum of Natural History Web site. Learn about the current threats to the species and find out about the measures being taken to save it.

EDITOR'S CHOICE

Access this Web site from http://www.myreportlinks.com

and South America, the caiman, a more aggressive crocodilian species when it comes to extending its habitat, has driven out the more docile American crocodile.

Commercial Hunting and Killing as Pests

Wildlife experts estimate that over the last fifty years, hunters have killed more than 20 million crocodilians worldwide. Their hunting meets people's demands for crocodilian meat and skins. No one is certain how many American crocodiles have been killed for their skins, which are used to make luggage, handbags, and shoes, but throughout the American crocodile's range, hunting for skins took a tremendous toll between 1930 and 1960. It was legal to hunt crocodiles in the United States until 1962. Fishermen throughout the Americas are also known to have killed crocodiles because they mistakenly believed that the animals depleted the fish population in estuaries.

Outside the United States, American crocodiles continued to be threatened by hunting and poaching, and they were still being killed as pests. This is an especially difficult problem to enforce after an animal has been killed, since the skin of a protected American crocodile closely resembles the skins of other crocodilians, such as the common caiman, which are not protected.

▷ Loss of Habitat in Florida

It is not known exactly how far and wide the American crocodile roamed in its historical range. But looking at habitat losses in the United States as an example, one can see that this endangered species has been steadily pushed into more and more remote wetlands by human population growth.

Between 1936 and 1987, one third of the forested land in South Florida was cleared for agriculture or for homes. During roughly that same period, South Florida's human population grew by more than 4.7 million people. American crocodile numbers continued to fall until just a

Eighty-five percent of the world's crocodiles have become endangered because of reptile product trade, including illegal trade in endangered crocodile hides. The Animal Welfare Institute reports on current efforts to stem this commerce.

Access this Web site from http://www.myreportlinks.com

few hundred of them remained by the early 1970s.[1]

Loss of habitat in Florida from Biscayne Bay northward and from Key Largo southward has driven the American crocodile from those areas. Human development of that habitat is the cause. A great deal of habitat has been lost due to the huge population growth in the Miami area. Where there once were vast tangles of mangrove forest, swamps were filled in. High-rise buildings, homes, strip malls, roads, resorts, marinas, shoreline bulkheads, and public beaches were built on top of them. People vacationing today in South Florida probably have no idea they are playing in sand

and surf that was once a vast mangrove swamp and home to the American crocodile.

It is this dramatic and permanent loss of habitat in Florida that makes it unlikely that the American crocodile population there will ever increase very much. The species has staked out nearly all the mangrove habitat remaining in the state.

American crocodile habitat has also declined in all the other countries in which it lives. Most of this habitat in Mexico, Central America, and South America has been lost to human encroachment as estuaries are filled in to make way for urbanization, agricultural land, cattle ranches, or beach

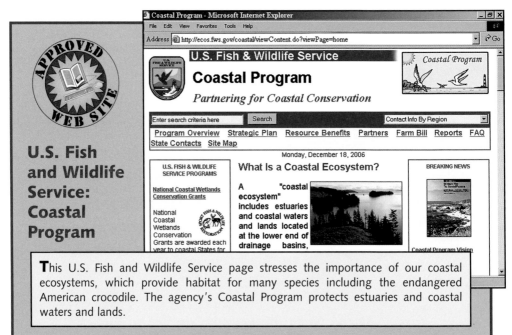

U.S. Fish and Wildlife Service: Coastal Program

This U.S. Fish and Wildlife Service page stresses the importance of our coastal ecosystems, which provide habitat for many species including the endangered American crocodile. The agency's Coastal Program protects estuaries and coastal waters and lands.

Access this Web site from http://www.myreportlinks.com

resorts. No studies have been done to assess the amount of habitat lost over the last century throughout the American crocodile's range.

Degradation of Habitat

Degradation of habitat is often difficult to see, but damage to the area in which animals live is especially harmful to endangered species. Degradation does not need to be as dramatic as the building of a highway or an airport for wildlife to be harmed. Habitat degradation can be as subtle as the addition of a few hundredths of a percent of salt to formerly freshwater, causing harm to crocodile hatchlings. It can also come from the introduction of a nonnative species, such as Australian pine. In Florida, that plant encroaches on the nests of the American crocodile.

The Perils of Pollution

Pollution also causes natural habitat to be degraded, although its effects may not be known for years or decades. Over the last thirty years, the Florida Everglades have been contaminated by large amounts of agricultural pesticides. When it rains, these chemicals are carried from farmlands into lakes and streams; they also enter the groundwater. Some pesticides in high enough concentrations can poison crocodiles and other animals. They also negatively affect species' ability to reproduce.

Mercury and pesticides are two pollutants that have already been found in crocodile eggs. When toxic chemicals such as those find their way into bodies of water, they pose a risk to the health of all animals that live in or near rivers, lakes, and oceans.

Mercury is another highly poisonous substance that may pose a threat to crocodiles, especially eggs and nestlings. Mercury, a heavy metal, is a pollutant that is emitted from coal-burning power plants and factories. It is carried on the wind and eventually settles into bodies of water and on land. The mercury then builds up in the food chain, so that the fish and amphibians eaten by crocodiles are contaminated with it.

Scientists have already found mercury and pesticides in the eggs of crocodiles. They do not yet know how much of these substances it will take to cause serious health problems for American crocodiles, but they are conducting research to find out.

Other Threats

Human encroachment is also a threat to the American crocodile. As recreational demands in-crease on public lands, activities such as camping, fishing, and boating all have a negative effect on the shy American crocodile. The use of recre-ational boats, including Jet Skis, has been limited in some of the areas of Everglades National Park where American crocodiles live.[2]

The Trouble With Salt

The natural environment of the American croco-dile carries its own difficulties for the species. The American crocodile is able to tolerate saltwater.

It has special glands that excrete, or get rid of, excess salt to reduce water loss in its body. However, hatchling crocodiles need freshwater to grow in, because they cannot tolerate high levels of salt. Hatchlings are known to become stressed and occasionally die during periods of low rainfall. During those periods, salt becomes more concentrated in the estuaries they live in.

When hatchlings leave their nests, they swim immediately into saltwater estuaries. Their survival rate in those estuaries for the first year can range from 6 percent to 50 percent, depending on the availability of sufficient freshwater.

Unfortunately, in the twentieth century, a lot of freshwater was diverted away from the Everglades

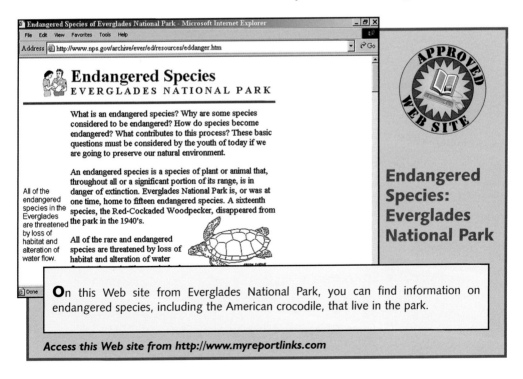

Endangered Species
EVERGLADES NATIONAL PARK

What is an endangered species? Why are some species considered to be endangered? How do species become endangered? What contributes to this process? These basic questions must be considered by the youth of today if we are going to preserve our natural environment.

An endangered species is a species of plant or animal that, throughout all or a significant portion of its range, is in danger of extinction. Everglades National Park is, or was at one time, home to fifteen endangered species. A sixteenth species, the Red-Cockaded Woodpecker, disappeared from the park in the 1940's.

All of the endangered species in the Everglades are threatened by loss of habitat and alteration of water flow.

All of the rare and endangered species are threatened by loss of habitat and alteration of water

Endangered Species: Everglades National Park

On this Web site from Everglades National Park, you can find information on endangered species, including the American crocodile, that live in the park.

Access this Web site from http://www.myreportlinks.com

to be used for agricultural lands, especially in citrus groves. As a result, water that was once fresh in Everglades National Park became increasingly salty, threatening crocodile hatchlings. An $8 billion government program is now under way to enhance the flow of freshwater back into the Everglades to restore the natural balance in its ecosystem, thereby helping endangered species. The future survival rates of American crocodile hatchlings will provide an important measure of how successful this freshwater restoration program is in the Everglades.

Highway Deaths

Crocodiles often die when they attempt to cross busy Florida roads. An average of three to four American crocodiles are killed each year while trying to cross U.S. Highway 1 and Card Sound Road in southern Florida. Fences have been installed to prevent such traffic fatalities, but they have not been effective in saving many crocodiles. In 1984, signs were placed along U.S. Highway 1 to improve public awareness, slow traffic, and reduce crocodile fatalities, but it remains to be seen whether drivers heed them.

Exotic Species

Exotic species, also called invasive species, are species of plants and animals that are not native to the area in which they are growing. Once they are introduced to a region, they tend to take over and drive out native species. In Florida, several exotic species of vegetation have been known to overrun American crocodile nesting sites.

On Florida's Key Largo, Australian pine, Malaysian cajeput, and Brazilian pepper have taken over levees and berms (banks and mounds) where crocodiles nest. These invasive species have also been found along the canals at Turkey Point and in Everglades National Park where crocodiles nest.

Fortunately, federal and state officials have developed a plan for controlling these invasive plants, and so far, those projects have been effective at holding the plants in check. Unfortunately, exotic species are nearly impossible to remove completely from an ecosystem once they have been introduced. So the spraying, cutting, and controlling of Australian pine and Brazilian pepper will probably have to continue indefinitely if American crocodile nests are to be permanently protected.

▶Climate Change

Climate change that results from global warming could have a major impact on the future of the American crocodile. If global warming causes glaciers in polar regions and elsewhere around the world to continue melting at a faster rate throughout this century, as seems likely to happen, then sea levels could rise significantly. Southern Florida and all the current habitat of the American crocodile there could eventually be flooded and completely covered by water—reclaimed by the sea. One computer modeling study shows that within just twenty years, 90 percent of Florida's flats, or shallow waters, could be flooded. By the year 2100, there could be only 1 percent remaining.[3] Such flats are currently key crocodile habitat.

Wildlife experts do not know if the American crocodile could migrate along receding shores. If it does migrate with changing coastlines, it will have to deal with the limitations imposed on it by urban shores dominated by cities, roads, docks, and wharves. This might be very difficult for the species.

The extreme weather, especially drought, that would come with climate change could also cause problems for the American crocodile. Extreme drought changes the ratio of saltwater to freshwater, and too much saltwater can harm American crocodile hatchlings. It is difficult to say whether extreme drought will occur across Central America and Florida in coming decades, although some climate models do

◁ Scientists believe that the current land habitat of the American crocodile could be covered by water in the future because of global warming. Places like Fort Lauderdale, Florida, where this photo was taken, would be one such place.

An American crocodile on a sandbar, photographed from above. Today, habitat loss and poaching are the biggest threats facing the American crocodile.

show that extreme drought could happen there as a result of climate change.

Climate models also show an increase in the intensity of hurricanes as a result of a global warming. It is not known what impact category-five hurricanes such as Hurricane Katrina might have on American crocodile habitat. It is known, however, that tidal surges, rough seas, and high winds can kill crocodiles while also eroding important nesting beaches. One study suggests that regularly occurring major hurricanes is what keeps Florida crocodile populations from growing significantly.[4]

▶ Rising Temperatures Bring Uncertain Future

Global warming may cause another problem for the American crocodile and some other reptiles, such as turtles and lizards. The sex of a crocodilian hatchling—whether it turns out to be male or female—is determined by the temperature at which an egg is incubated inside the nest. This is called temperature-dependent sex determination (TSD). Studies have shown that nest temperatures higher than 90 to 93°F (32 to 34°C) produce a clutch of male American alligators. Temperatures lower than 82 to 86°F (28 to 30°C) produce all females. Temperatures between those two extremes produce mixed clutches of females and males. Precise TSD statistics have not been calculated for the American crocodile, but scientists know that the sex of its hatchlings depend on temperature. United Nations scientists estimate that by the year 2100, emissions of greenhouse gases into the atmosphere (such as carbon dioxide released through fuel burned by cars and other vehicles) could raise the average temperatures around the world as much as 2.5 to 10.4°F (1.4 to 5.8°C). The effect that this increase might have on crocodilian eggs is unknown, but it could cause many more males than females to be born—or the animals could somehow adapt to the heat. Scientists do know that crocodilian species have survived through periods of natural global warming over the past 200 million years.

It may be possible for the American crocodile to actually thrive in a warmer world, extending its range along the coasts of North and South America, but at this point, no one knows. We will all have to wait and see how climate change affects this species and other endangered species.

PROTECTING THE AMERICAN CROCODILE

Unfortunately, only the United States, Costa Rica, and Venezuela have adequately protected the American crocodile and its habitat, and it is only in South Florida that the species' numbers have rebounded. Cuba has also made some effort to preserve its crocodiles by creating a few protected areas for them. Other countries in this

American Crocodile

ARKive is a digital library that holds hundreds of images of endangered and threatened animals as well as movies, distribution maps, and discussions of range, habitat, and biology. Included are images of the American crocodile.

Access this Web site from http://www.myreportlinks.com

endangered species' range, however, have limited or ineffective laws to protect it. Many countries are having trouble enforcing their own laws to protect American crocodiles.

The Endangered Species Act

The American crocodile was listed and protected under the U.S. Endangered Species Act (ESA) on September 25, 1975. At the time, there were only about ten to twenty breeding female American crocodiles remaining in all of Florida.

Protection under the ESA led to regularly up-dated recovery plans for the American crocodile. The current plan calls for the protection of most of the critical habitat for all life stages of the animal. It also includes plans to conduct research on the crocodile's life cycle and educate the public about the value of the American crocodile to the Florida ecosystem. It is the successful implementation of this plan that most biologists credit for the recovery of the American crocodile in Florida. Most important to the species' recovery has been the protection of about 87 percent of crocodile critical habitat in South Florida.

CITES and the IUCN Red List

A large step was taken to protect the American crocodile when most of the countries in its range joined what is now called the IUCN-World Conservation Union, the largest conservation network in the world. (The IUCN is the International Union for the Conservation of Nature and Natural Resources.) Member nations, known as parties, agree to abide by the rules of the Convention on International Trade in Endangered Species of Wild Fauna and Flora (CITES).

CITES is an international agreement between governments to ensure that the trade of wild animals and plants does not harm their survival. The American crocodile was listed as an Appendix I species on June 6, 1981, meaning that it is given full protection from international commerce. The CITES treaty has led to a sharp

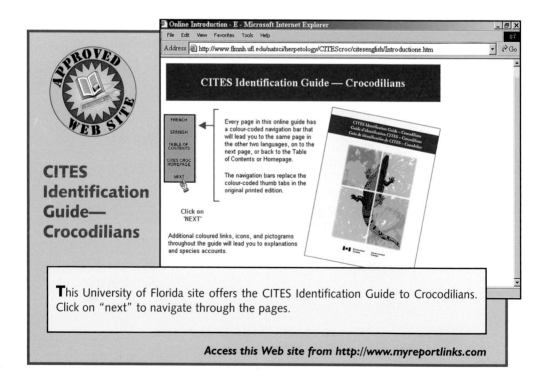

CITES Identification Guide— Crocodilians

This University of Florida site offers the CITES Identification Guide to Crocodilians. Click on "next" to navigate through the pages.

Access this Web site from http://www.myreportlinks.com

decline in the trading of American crocodile skins—though illegal trade is known to still occur. Currently the IUCN Red List, a list of endangered and threatened species worldwide, lists the American crocodile as "vulnerable" to extinction, a step below endangered.

Individual Responsibility

As important as the ESA and CITES are to preserving endangered and threatened species, individual countries are still responsible for protecting the wildlife within their own borders. A few other countries have taken vital steps to begin protecting the American crocodile. Mexico, for example, has outlawed all crocodile hunting. Cuba has set up no-hunting zones in parts of the country. Venezuela and Costa Rica have also moved toward fully protecting their American crocodiles.

It is difficult to enforce environmental laws in many developing nations, however, especially in those places where the people are really poor and have few opportunities to make a better living. In some of those places, they still harvest the American crocodile just to feed their families. Until alternative ways of making a living are found for such people, the poaching and hunting of the American crocodile will continue.

▶Refuges in the United States: The Everglades

The survival of the American crocodile depends on the preservation and protection of its habitat. This effort has been particularly successful in the United States.

The federal government took the first major step toward protecting the American crocodile's last refuges almost thirty years before the crocodile was declared an endangered species. On December 6, 1947, President Harry S Truman formally dedicated Everglades National Park, protecting "the spectacular plant and animal life that distinguishes this place from all others in our country."[1]

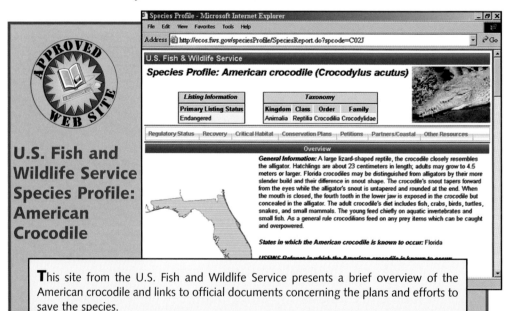

U.S. Fish and Wildlife Service Species Profile: American Crocodile

This site from the U.S. Fish and Wildlife Service presents a brief overview of the American crocodile and links to official documents concerning the plans and efforts to save the species.

Access this Web site from http://www.myreportlinks.com

The 1,509,000-acre park came just in time for the American crocodile. Had the Everglades been developed as citrus groves or cattle ranches, the crocodile would probably not have recovered. Today, Everglades National Park provides refuge to fifteen endangered species—including butterflies, rodents, mammals, birds, reptiles, and amphibians. In addition to providing a home for the American crocodile, it also provides habitat for four species of sea turtle, the red-cockaded woodpecker, the West Indian manatee, and the Florida panther.

The American crocodile can often be seen by tourists visiting the park. According to Paul Moler, a wildlife biologist with the Florida Fish and Wildlife Conservation Commission, "Go to Flamingo in Everglades National Park and you can see American crocodiles in the water. . . . At the marina there are a couple large crocs that hang out and you tend to see them basking [in the sun]. When out basking, crocs typically bask with the mouth open, alligators with the mouth closed."[2]

▶ Other Protected Areas

Another major federal preserve was established in 1980 to protect the American crocodile and its critical habitat. The 6,606-acre Crocodile Lake National Wildlife Refuge is located in Monroe County, Florida. The refuge covers a significant portion of north Key Largo and is the primary home of American crocodiles in the Florida Keys. The area includes undisturbed man-made channels and 4,213 acres of mangrove forest that are popular with the crocodiles. Because the refuge's primary purpose is for the study and protection of endangered species, it is closed to the public. Scientists appreciate this reserve because it allows them to study the timid American crocodile in the wild without any human disturbances. This is especially important during the March to October breeding season when females are guarding their nests. Female crocodiles are known to completely abandon their nests after just a single human disturbance.

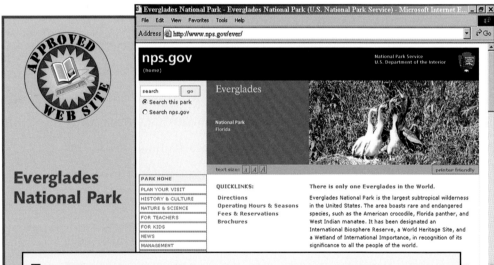

Everglades National Park

The Web site for Everglades National Park includes information about the endangered species that are protected within the park's unique ecosystem, including the American crocodile.

Access this Web site from http://www.myreportlinks.com

American crocodile habitat has been protected elsewhere in Florida, including Biscayne National Park, J. N. "Ding" Darling National Wildlife Refuge, Ten Thousand Islands National Wildlife Refuge, Collier-Seminole State Park, Dagny Johnson Key Largo Hammock Botanical State Park, and several Miami-Dade County parks. Florida also offers another significant protection for the American crocodile: All mangrove forests within the state are now protected, even ones on private property.

While not enough American crocodile habitat has been protected in other parts of its range outside the United States, there are some success stories. Santa Rosa National Park in Costa Rica and Morrocoy National Park in Venezuela have American crocodile populations. If this endangered species is to survive and thrive outside of the United States, similar parks in other parts of the American crocodile's range will need to be set aside.

▷ A Government-Corporate Partnership That Works

Government efforts to protect endangered species often conflict with the business of private corporations, which is to earn profits. This has not been the case with the American crocodile. In fact, government and corporate interests are working together in a unique partnership to protect the species.

Florida Power & Light Company, which provides electrical service to about half of the state's population, generates some of its power from nuclear sources. One of those nuclear power plants is Turkey Point, in southeastern Florida. Strangely enough, it has been the site of one of the American crocodile's best-protected habitats for more than twenty-five years. American crocodile hatchlings were first found to be living in the company's 5,900-acre system of cooling canals in 1978. The canals provide ideal nesting sites for the reptiles. This critical nesting habitat in the cooling-canal system has been responsible for most of the population increase of the American crocodile over the past couple of decades.

▶ A Powerful Ally

The company not only allows the crocodiles to nest and live in its cooling canals, but it has also developed a sophisticated management plan with the aid of state and federal governments to help the crocodiles thrive. Florida Power & Light seeks regular input from the U.S. Fish and Wildlife Service and the Florida Fish and Wildlife Conservation Commission in the development of its American crocodile recovery plan. Working in cooperation with those groups, it monitors the

animals in the entire 150 miles of its canals.
Intensive surveys are conducted both night and
day during and between nesting seasons in
which American crocodile hatchlings are counted
and tagged.

Observers have counted an increase in the
number of crocodile nests and hatchlings at
Turkey Point. Only one or two nests and thirty
hatchlings were seen each year in the late 1970s,
but there were seventeen known nests and more
than three hundred hatchlings in 2003. There

The Crocodile's Power Play - National Wildlife Magazine - Microsoft Internet Explorer

File   Edit   View   Favorites   Tools   Help

Address http://www.nwf.org/nationalwildlife/article.cfm?articleId=493&issueId=40   Go

Crocodile hatchlings emerge from their shells. Some American crocodiles have
found an unusual place to nest: the berms of the cooling canals of the Florida
Power & Light Company's Turkey Point Plant. **"The Crocodile's Power Play,"**
an online article from the magazine of the National Wildlife Federation,
examines the American crocodile's ability to adapt to changing habitats.

have been more than three thousand hatchling crocodiles counted in all at the Turkey Point site.[3]

Florida Power & Light has enhanced crocodile habitat by constructing freshwater refuges for hatchlings, removing exotic vegetation (such as Australian pines) from nesting areas, relocating hatchlings to more suitable habitat to protect them from predators, and coordinating maintenance activities to ensure the crocodiles' safety. The company has even hired a staff crocodilian expert to manage the program.

▷ Crocodile Experts

The most extensive studies of the American crocodile have been conducted in Florida, at major universities. The American crocodile research and recovery program, underway since 1975, has also been better funded than similar programs outside the United States. Research findings from the United States are made available to developing nations interested in protecting the American crocodiles in their countries.

Two of the leading scientists studying American crocodiles in the United States are Frank Mazzotti, a wildlife ecologist with the University of Florida, and Paul Moler, a wildlife biologist with the Florida Fish and Wildlife Conservation Commission. Since the 1970s, they have added much to the knowledge we have of this endangered species.

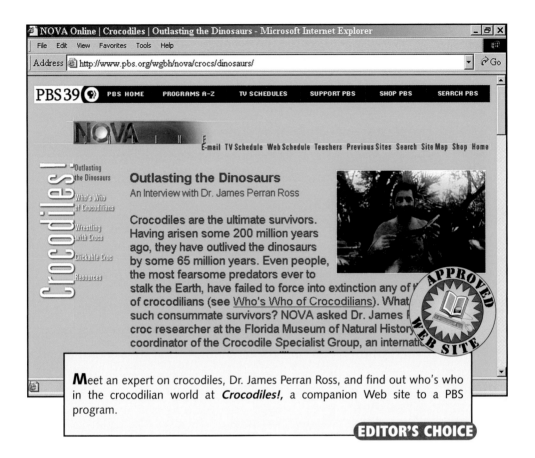

NOVA

E-mail TV Schedule Web Schedule Teachers Previous Sites Search Site Map Shop Home

Outlasting
the Dinosaurs

Who's Who
of Crocodilians

Wrestling
with Crocs

Clickable Croc

Resources

Outlasting the Dinosaurs
An Interview with Dr. James Perran Ross

Crocodiles are the ultimate survivors.
Having arisen some 200 million years
ago, they have outlived the dinosaurs
by some 65 million years. Even people,
the most fearsome predators ever to
stalk the Earth, have failed to force into extinction any of t
of crocodilians (see Who's Who of Crocodilians). What
such consummate survivors? NOVA asked Dr. James
croc researcher at the Florida Museum of Natural Histor
coordinator of the Crocodile Specialist Group, an internati

APPROVED WEB SITE

Meet an expert on crocodiles, Dr. James Perran Ross, and find out who's who
in the crocodilian world at **Crocodiles!**, a companion Web site to a PBS
program.

EDITOR'S CHOICE

Both crocodile experts have also tried to educate the public about the American crocodile's importance to its ecosystem. They have attempted to do this by stressing the species' shyness. According to Moler, "There's a pervasive misconception that crocodiles are more aggressive than alligators." He is quick to point out that although alligator attacks are well documented, "There's never been a documented crocodile attack; they are pretty much reclusive animals."[4]

Mazzotti and Moler agree that the American crocodile is now safe enough in Florida to down-list the species to threatened. Their work shows, however, that the American crocodile still faces problems, especially if adequate freshwater flow is not restored to the Everglades in coming years.

Sustainable Use

One model for preserving crocodilians in the developing world that has worked well with other species is sustainable use—a responsible use of resources at a rate that meets present-day needs while conserving resources for future generations. Crocodilians can be used sustainably in several ways: through the controlled hunting of wild crocodilians; ranching, or bringing eggs or hatchlings from the wild and raising them in captivity; and captive breeding, or farming, by maintaining breeding adults in captivity and raising their offspring. Controlled sustainable use of American crocodiles takes pressure off the species in the wild, reducing the number of animals hunted or poached.

Commercial captive breeding of the American crocodile for its skin is being done in the Central American country of Honduras. The legal facility there holds about four hundred breeding stock and regularly produces offspring. In Colombia, four commercial facilities hold a total of 439

An old image of a crocodile being skinned for its hide, which is still in demand in some places to make belts, shoes, and purses. While it is illegal to kill American crocodiles in the wild, commercial captive breeding of the American crocodile for its skin is not.

breeders and more than 9,000 juvenile crocodiles produced in farms. In 2001, one hundred American crocodile skins were legally shipped from Colombia's sustainable crocodile farms to France. This was the first legal trading of the species since 1989.[5] There are also successful captive-breeding facilities in Cuba, Panama, and Peru, but their production levels are low.

The Role of Ecotourism

In the United States, sustainable uses such as hunting or captive breeding are not allowed under the Endangered Species Act. Sustainable use through ecotourism, however, is encouraged. In Florida, tourism has a greater impact on the state's economy than any other industry, and the state's natural resources have drawn people for many years. It is only fairly recently, though, that eco-tourism has been promoted in Florida as widely as it is now. This responsible travel to natural places aimed at helping to sustain both wildlife and the economy is aided by the American crocodile, found in the Flamingo area of Everglades National Park and other sites around the state.

In Florida, ecotourism is one way to encourage the many vacationers in the Sunshine State to experience more than a theme park or a beach. There is a delicate balancing act, however, in attracting visitors to natural places. Even the most well-planned tourism can overwhelm a unique ecosystem like the Everglades, the only place in the world where alligators and crocodiles coexist. So, the challenge in promoting ecotourism is to make sure that the natural resources themselves are not being harmed by the people they are attracting.

CURRENT STATUS AND CONSERVATION EFFORTS

Though the American crocodile is the most widespread crocodile species in the Americas, its numbers have been reduced by habitat loss, habitat degradation, and many decades of commercial exploitation through hunting and poaching. Populations are small and declining throughout the species' range in North, Central, and South America. It is only in Florida that the species has now rebounded, and its numbers seem stable. The total number of American crocodiles in the world is currently estimated to be between 10,000 and 20,000, with as many as 1,200 of those in Florida.

Some local populations have been wiped out, and poaching for American crocodile hides outside the United States continues to pose a major threat. Most populations of American crocodiles are small, isolated, and in remote areas that are relatively inaccessible to people. Scientists who study the American crocodile expect the species to continue to decline severely and rapidly in the near future throughout most of its range.

The American crocodile has rebounded in Florida thanks to a cooperative effort by federal, state, and local governments as well as private citizens. This photograph of an American crocodile was taken in Everglades National Park, home to fifteen endangered species.

▶ The Species' Status Worldwide

The Status Survey and Conservation Action Plan for Crocodiles, published in 1992 and revised in 1998 by the IUCN/SSC Crocodile Specialist Group, provides a summary of the current status of the world's twenty-three crocodilian species. It also contains an updated plan of action to conserve those species that are endangered or vulnerable. The following summarizes the portion of that report dealing with the American crocodile.

According to the IUCN, most survey data for the American crocodile is poor. No recent American crocodile population surveys are available from El Salvador, Guatemala, Panama, Colombia, Ecuador, or Peru. Some data is available from the other countries where the species lives, but it is only in the United States that thorough research and surveying has taken place. Eight countries in which the American crocodile lives offer complete protection to the species by law, but few enforce these laws very effectively. El Salvador and Haiti have no American crocodile management programs. Five countries are actively farming the American crocodile, a first step toward protection of the species. Farming is planned to begin in Jamaica as well. American crocodiles are currently being raised on ranches in Cuba.

Crocodile Conservation Program

The Wildlife Conservation Society is actively involved in supporting worldwide research and conservation programs for crocodilians. Read more about its efforts at the WCS Web site.

Access this Web site from http://www.myreportlinks.com

▶ The American Crocodile in Mexico and Central America

Surveys found American crocodiles in Mexico living in the Santiago River in the states of Nayarit and Jalisco. However, the crocodiles there may be threatened by dam-building projects. American crocodile populations in the Mexican states of Sinaloa, Yucatán, and Veracruz are greatly reduced or extinct.

Scientists have also found that there are few American crocodiles left in Guatemala. The good news there, however, is that a private conservation program is helping to maintain a captive-breeding stock of American crocodiles.

A dwarf caiman. This crocodile species, found in semiaquatic regions of Central and South America, is not endangered.

In Honduras, a small number of American crocodiles are thought to live in most of the rivers flowing into the Caribbean Sea, though they may be extinct in some of these. The IUCN reports, however, that one population in El Cajon reservoir has been negatively affected by human action and by changes in water levels.

Belize is one of the few places where the species is doing well, although development on the coast has reduced habitat. Even though protected by law in Belize, crocodiles are still lost to poaching, accidental drowning in fishing nets, and

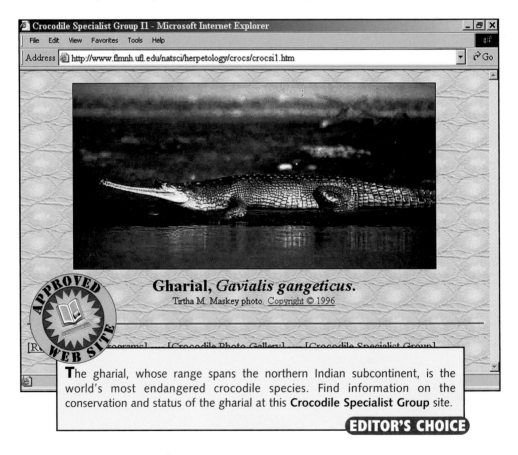

Gharial, *Gavialis gangeticus.*
Tirtha M. Maskey photo. Copyright © 1996

The gharial, whose range spans the northern Indian subcontinent, is the world's most endangered crocodile species. Find information on the conservation and status of the gharial at this **Crocodile Specialist Group** site.

EDITOR'S CHOICE

habitat destruction, especially the destruction of critical nesting places.

Researchers in Nicaragua say that the American crocodile is "very rare but still present" along rivers and bays draining into the Caribbean Sea. American crocodiles are also found along that country's Pacific Coast and near Managua, the capital city. Nicaraguans sometimes illegally kill the protected American crocodile at the same time that they are legally hunting for caiman, a crocodilian whose hide closely resembles that of the American crocodile.

In Costa Rica, there are more than three hundred American crocodiles in the Rio Grande de Tárcoles, a river that drains into the Pacific, and another thirty-five in Estero Roto, a wetland resembling an estuary. The animals are also found in Costa Rica's Playa Nancite, a beach. They are rare but have been seen in major rivers feeding the Caribbean Sea.

Caribbean Crocodile Populations

The American crocodile inhabits six mainland locations and eleven Caribbean cays, or islands. A population of American crocodiles living in and around a landlocked saltwater lake in the southwestern Dominican Republic has been intensely studied and surveyed. The conservation of American crocodiles living in Lago Enriquillo, the largest natural lake in the Dominican Republic, is a true success story. By 1992, the crocodile population there had been reduced to about one third of its size in the 1980s through illegal killing and a decreased food supply. After a program to protect the crocodiles was begun, the population increased and is now believed to be stable, at about 200.

Significant numbers of American crocodiles inhabit Cuba's Zapata swamp and live on Isla de Juventud ("Island of Youth"), the Canarreos Archipelago, the Jobabo and Cheve lagoon, and the Birama swamp.

The Situation in South America

There have been few surveys of the American crocodile population in Colombia, so little is known about their numbers in that South American country. However, large populations that once inhabited the Atlantic Coast are thought to be diminished or extinct. Colombians are helping the American crocodile by raising stocks through captive breeding.

In Ecuador, the destruction of coastal mangrove swamps and their replacement by shrimp aquaculture centers has ruined a lot of crocodile habitat. A few American crocodiles are in captivity there, and it is hoped that they can someday be bred and restored to the wild.

In northeastern Peru, the southernmost limit of the American crocodile's range, small numbers of animals have been found in the mangrove swamps and mouths of the Tumbes, Mango, Tigre, Ucumares, and Chica rivers.

In Venezuela, surveys suggest that some populations are stable or even growing because they have been protected and supplemented by restocking of ranch-raised crocodiles. Some animals are still being killed illegally, however, for medicinal purposes.

Cooperation among countries and continued efforts to address the needs of people and animals so that both benefit are recommendations of *The Status Survey and Conservation Action Plan.* There is hope for *Crocodylus acutus.* As the report

Promise for the Survival of the Orinoco Crocodile: a strong commitment from the private sector - Micros...

File   Edit   View   Favorites   Tools   Help

Address http://www.tortoisereserve.org/Research/Croc_Article_Body2.html   Go

Promise for the Survival of the Orinoco Crocodile: a strong commitment from the private sector in Venezuela

In 1800 the German scientist Alexander von Humboldt spent four months exploring the then wild and uninhabited Orinoco. He traveled 1,725 miles of the vast northern South American river's basin. Humboldt wrote vivid accounts of his encounters with huge numbers of crocodiles, many of which exceeded 6 meters (20 feet) in length.

Most of the stock animals come from the ranch itself, but some from other ranches in the Llanos are purchased or donated. A large butchering area with tile tables and scales for weighing food are adjacent to the freezer. Pedro Azuaje, the farms manager, and the person responsible for overseeing the program, estimates his adult crocs consume 14,300 kg of food a year. A separate incubation building was constructed for the crocodile eggs. The eggs are incubated in damp sand warmed by suspended heat lamps, and the floor of the building is flooded throughout the incubation period (the dry season) to keep the humidity high

APPROVED WEB SITE

Promise for the Survival of the Orinoco Crocodile

Done

The Orinoco crocodile is an endangered freshwater crocodile in Venezuela. This site describes some of the efforts by a private group called the Tortoise Reserve to save the species from extinction.

Access this Web site from http://www.myreportlinks.com

states, "[Because] American crocodiles produce a commercially valuable hide, sustainable use programs based on ranching and farming are possible. But the development of management programs based on sustainable use must be approached on a country-by-country basis and be linked to the health of wild populations of American crocodiles."[1]

What You Can Do to Help the American Crocodile

The first step in helping to save any endangered species is to learn as much as you can about it and then share your knowledge with others. One place to begin learning about the American crocodile is to read more about the species by linking to the recommended Web sites on the MyReportLinks.com Web site. You can also find interesting books about the American crocodile listed on the Further Reading page of this book.

If your family is planning a vacation to Florida in the near future, you may want to encourage them to include a trip to the Everglades. There, you and your family could get a firsthand look at the mangrove swamps in which the American crocodile makes its home. A trip to Flamingo, deep in the heart of the Everglades, may even reward you with a look at *Crocodylus acutus* in its native environment, basking in the sun.

An interest in the American crocodile and other endangered species could even lead to a career in wildlife biology in which you could one day actively participate in saving animals at risk from extinction. Wildlife biologists Frank Mazzotti and Paul Moler have been instrumental in conserving the American crocodile. They survey, mark, weigh, and measure the animals, and try to learn more about their life cycle. They also write reports that inform elected officials how best to protect the American crocodile.

▶ **Organize a Preservation Campaign**

Whether or not you decide to make saving endangered animals your life's work, you can begin to

Survival in the Everglades

Crocodiles feed on small fish, invertebrates, reptiles, birds and mammals. Feeding and growth rates vary with temperature, food availability, and salinity. Diminished freshwater flow to Ever- glades estuaries have negatively affected growth rates of crocodiles.

Occasionally, deaths result from direct or indirect interactions with man, such as collisions with cars. Crocodiles also die from fatal wounds inflicted by other crocodiles or from cannibalism. Survival rates are the lowest for hatchlings, which are faced with many threats from predators

The American Crocodile: A Story of Recovery

The "Croc Docs," University of Florida scientists involved in the conservation of the American crocodile in Florida, profile the species' recovery. Charts, photographs, maps, and diagrams help explain the crocodile's current status.

EDITOR'S CHOICE

Access this Web site from http://www.myreportlinks.com

help those species by organizing a campaign to educate others about their plight. There are many ways to organize an American crocodile education and advocacy campaign.

What to Include

With your class, put together a presentation at your school to inform others about the threats to the American crocodile. Even if you do not live in Florida, the environment in your own state probably suffers from many of the same problems that affect crocodile habitat. These include the struggle to control urban and suburban sprawl, the loss of vital wildlife habitat, mercury and other forms of toxic pollution, and animal collisions with cars and trucks. You may want to compare these problems in your own "territory" with the problems suffered by the American crocodile in its territory.

You can also organize a class letter-writing campaign in which you urge elected officials and government wildlife agencies to take action to protect the American crocodile and other endangered species. In your letters, you might ask federal officials as well as those in Florida to work toward controlling suburban sprawl in the state, to increase funding for American crocodile research and recovery, and to cut mercury emissions from power plants.

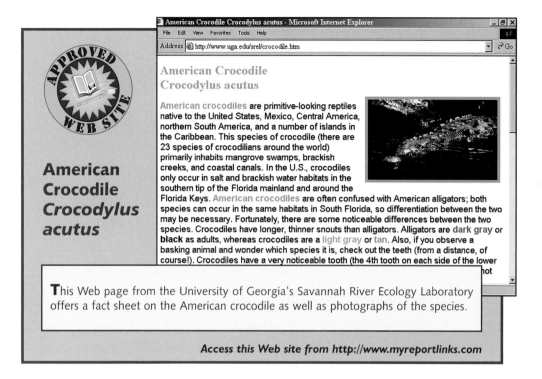

American
Crocodile
*Crocodylus
acutus*

American Crocodile
Crocodylus acutus

American crocodiles are primitive-looking reptiles native to the United States, Mexico, Central America, northern South America, and a number of islands in the Caribbean. This species of crocodile (there are 23 species of crocodilians around the world) primarily inhabits mangrove swamps, brackish creeks, and coastal canals. In the U.S., crocodiles only occur in salt and brackish water habitats in the southern tip of the Florida mainland and around the Florida Keys. American crocodiles are often confused with American alligators; both species can occur in the same habitats in South Florida, so differentiation between the two may be necessary. Fortunately, there are some noticeable differences between the two species. Crocodiles have longer, thinner snouts than alligators. Alligators are dark gray or black as adults, whereas crocodiles are a light gray or tan. Also, if you observe a basking animal and wonder which species it is, check out the teeth (from a distance, of course!). Crocodiles have a very noticeable tooth (the 4th tooth on each side of the lower

This Web page from the University of Georgia's Savannah River Ecology Laboratory offers a fact sheet on the American crocodile as well as photographs of the species.

Access this Web site from http://www.myreportlinks.com

▶ Help Protect the Endangered Species Act

The Endangered Species Act has been a tremendous success since its passage more than thirty years ago. It has helped bring back the American eagle, the symbol of our nation. It has also helped animals such as the green sea turtle and grizzly bear to survive. But in recent years, some large corporations and developers have launched a campaign to undermine the act's effectiveness—or do away with it altogether.

▶ Wisdom or Folly?

This loosely knit group has come to be called the "wise use movement," but environmentalists claim its intent is anything but wise. This group's philosophy is based on humans needing natural resources to survive, and a belief that the earth is not a fragile place but one whose resources are nearly infinite. In this view, the land, water, animals, and plants of the earth are to be used for our good, whether these wild places or wildlife survive or not. Some of the diverse industries that make up this movement include the mining, drilling, and timber industries; agriculture and grazing concerns; and the recreation and development industries.

In 2005, the U.S. House of Representatives passed the Threatened and Endangered Species

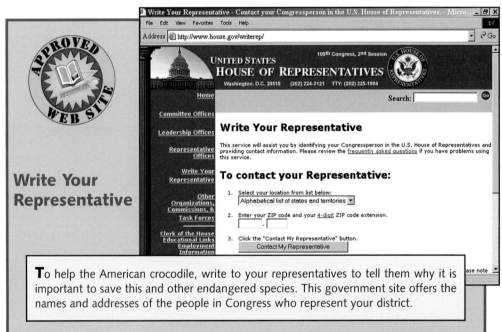

Write Your Representative

To help the American crocodile, write to your representatives to tell them why it is important to save this and other endangered species. This government site offers the names and addresses of the people in Congress who represent your district.

Access this Web site from http://www.myreportlinks.com

Recovery Act. The bill would do away with the "critical habitat" section of the Endangered Species Act and weaken it in other ways. If this bill or one like it is passed by the Senate and approved by the president, it will become law—and environmentalists will find it nearly impossible to continue protecting endangered species such as the American crocodile.

With your class, draft a letter to be sent to your representatives in Congress as well as to the president. In your letter, urge them not to allow the Endangered Species Act, the most far-reaching environmental law in history, to be weakened. Emphasize the importance of critical habit to the act's usefulness: It was the preservation of 87 percent of the American crocodile's critical habitat in Florida that helped it to recover there. The wise use movement is determined to get rid of the critical habitat provisions of the Endangered Species Act.

Chapter 6

CHANCES FOR SURVIVAL AND RECOVERY

Since its listing as an endangered species, the United States' population of American crocodiles has more than doubled—from between 100 and 400 animals in 1975 to between 500 and 1,200 today, a tremendous achievement.

Most crocodile experts credit this recovery to the remarkable success of the Endangered Species Act in focusing on the animal and on the protection of most of its critical habitat. "Endangered species designation spurred research, land acquisition and habitat management, all of which have contributed to [the unprecedented recovery of] this endangered species," says Dr. Frank Mazzotti.[1]

Elsewhere in its range, where the American crocodile lacks the strong protections offered by the Endangered Species Act, it is not doing nearly as well. In many areas, only general estimates exist of the numbers of individual crocs still surviving.

If the American crocodile is to survive throughout its range, the successful practices of the Endangered Species Act should be adopted by other nations. First, much better data is needed so that experts have a clearer idea of just how many American crocodiles actually exist throughout their range. Then, management plans need to be developed and enforced in each nation so that the American crocodile has a chance to recover in each country.

A Difficult and Uncertain Future

Recovering American crocodile populations in the United States do not mean the species will fare as well elsewhere. According to Paul Moler,

ADW: 28americancroc-5alt.jpg - Microsoft Internet Explorer

File   Edit   View   Favorites   Tools   Help

Address http://animaldiversity.ummz.umich.edu/site/resources/jerry_gingerich/28americancroc-5alt.jpg/view.html   Go

An important part of the effort to save the American crocodile depends upon learning as much as possible about the species. **Animal Diversity Web: Crocodylus acutus**, a site from the University of Michigan's Museum of Zoology, provides detailed information on the American crocodile and photographs of the reptiles.

EDITOR'S CHOICE

"Unfortunately, the proposal to down-list the American crocodile from endangered to threatened applies only to the U.S. population." Elsewhere in its range, the American crocodile is still struggling against human intrusions into its habitat. As Moler sums up, "There are areas where populations are secure and others not."[2]

Prognosis Outside the United States: The Good and Not-So-Good News

The IUCN-World Conservation Union crocodilian action plan lists projects it considers the most important for the species' recovery in other countries and rates places according to the likelihood that the species can actually recover there. As far as the

A glossary of terms, videos, photographs, and range maps are just some of the highlights of this Web page on crocodiles and alligators from the San Diego Zoo.

Access this Web site from http://www.myreportlinks.com

American crocodile is concerned, some places are better equipped than others to help the species.

Cuba and Belize are thought to be the places with the greatest opportunity for the species to recover because both provide habitat that is the least likely to be disturbed by humans. If Venezuela continues its conservation and restocking efforts, the species should continue to do well there. Costa Rica's conservation history makes it, too, a good place to conduct more research on American crocodiles' ability to recover. Jamaica is home to some abundant populations of American crocodiles, but a management plan to help these wild populations is still needed. Mexico needs a more coordinated effort throughout the crocodile's range to ensure its survival there. In Colombia, where American crocodile populations were once spread along both coasts, commercial trade in the reptiles' hide has depleted the population. The IUCN recommends a captive-breeding program there as well as population surveys. In Panama, Ecuador, El Salvador, Guatemala, Honduras, Haiti, and Peru, basic surveys are still needed, but scientists think that very few American crocodiles still exist there.[3]

▷ American Crocodile Stability in Florida

Even though the American crocodile is doing well enough in Florida for the U.S. Fish and Wildlife

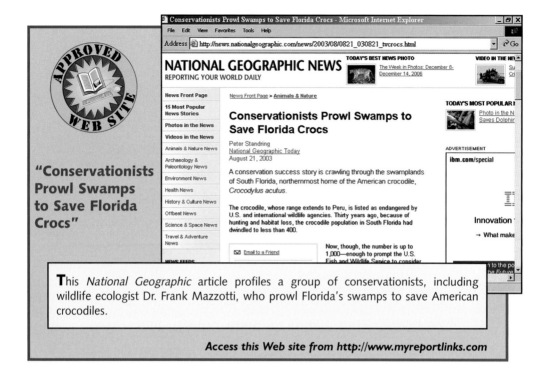

"Conservationists Prowl Swamps to Save Florida Crocs"

This *National Geographic* article profiles a group of conservationists, including wildlife ecologist Dr. Frank Mazzotti, who prowl Florida's swamps to save American crocodiles.

Access this Web site from http://www.myreportlinks.com

Service to consider down-listing the species, threats remain. According to Frank Mazzotti, "The problem now in Florida is not going to be loss of habitat, which is fully protected, but degradation of that protected habitat from *within,* because of human activities from *without.*"[4] Scientists are especially worried about the continued rapid development of coastal areas, which affects the freshwater flow to the estuaries where crocodiles and their hatchlings live. "If you lose the freshwater flow then you lose the suitability of the habitat for crocodiles," according to Mazzotti.[5] And that means you lose the crocodiles themselves.

SCIENCE, SANCTUARY, AND SUSTAINABILITY

If the American crocodile is to be permanently saved throughout its range, major steps need to be taken now.

The type of thorough scientific surveys carried out in Florida need to be conducted in other countries within the crocodile's range. Scientists need to locate populations of American crocodiles throughout their range and count them in order to establish baseline population data—the number of individuals in existence on a particular starting date. They then need to break down this data into the numbers of breeding adults, juveniles, hatchlings, ratios of females to males, and survival rates. Once this baseline data is gathered, it needs to be tracked over a number of years to determine the stability of the population, to see if it is growing or shrinking.

At the same time that populations are being counted, habitat loss and habitat degradation factors must be examined to see what the major threats are to the American crocodile in each

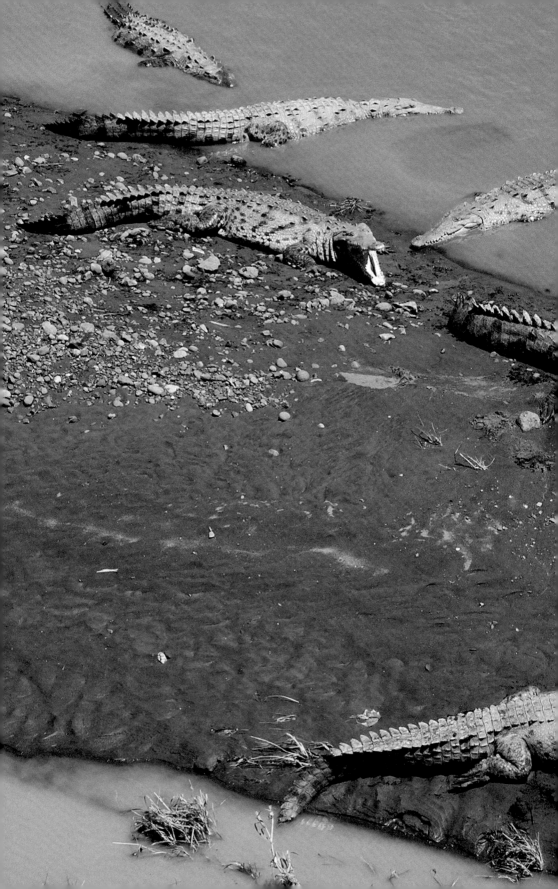

If American crocodiles like these are to continue to survive, we must all play a part in their recovery.

region. The life history of the animals must also be studied in order to better understand how they can more effectively breed and be protected.

Strategies for Saving Crocodiles

Good science is just the beginning. The next step is to develop a management plan for recovering and protecting the species in each of the countries where it lives. Questions such as the following need answers: What parts of the American crocodile's habitat are critical to its survival? Can these critical habitats be protected without depriving local peoples of their livelihoods? Where will the money and support for preservation come from?

One strategy to protect the American crocodile involves sustainable harvesting practices like those conducted with other crocodilians around the world. But the American crocodile's numbers would have to increase a lot before such sustainable harvesting would be commercially profitable and acceptable on a large scale.

The greatest challenge to the species is that much of its range is in developing countries that lack the money needed for conservation. It is not inexpensive to dedicate research for an endangered species. If the American crocodile is to survive throughout its range, then the successful strategies that have been employed in the United States under the Endangered Species Act need to

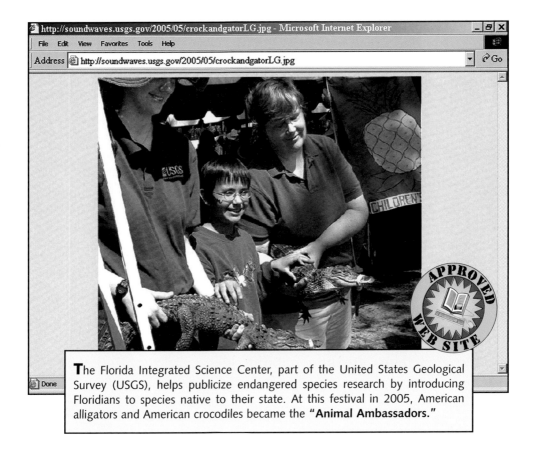

The Florida Integrated Science Center, part of the United States Geological Survey (USGS), helps publicize endangered species research by introducing Floridians to species native to their state. At this festival in 2005, American alligators and American crocodiles became the **"Animal Ambassadors."**

be extended to other nations where the animals' numbers are declining rapidly.

The greatest hurdle to permanent recovery of this species may still be the animal's negative image. Some people even think the world would be a better place if all crocodiles were driven from existence. Education is key to changing that perception of the ancient species. A U.S. Fish and Wildlife pamphlet about the American crocodile says it best:

We need to educate concerned citizens that the American crocodile is a shy animal that rarely attacks unless provoked. . . . Education promoting the tolerance and understanding of crocodile behavior and habitat has assisted in the survival of crocodiles throughout the world. We should not allow ungrounded fears and lack of awareness to interfere with the recovery of the American crocodile. It is possible to co-exist peacefully with crocodiles if people are ready to embrace the responsibility to protect an endangered species.[1]

The success of American crocodile recovery in Florida should not lure us into thinking that we do not need to do more to save this species. The future—with its threats of global climate change, further habitat loss, and continued habitat degradation—is still uncertain for the American crocodile. Only our ongoing concern, advocacy, and action will permanently protect this endangered species.

In 1973, Congress took the farsighted step of creating the Endangered Species Act, widely regarded as the world's strongest and most effective wildlife conservation law. It set an ambitious goal: to reverse the alarming trend of human-caused extinction that threatened the ecosystems we all share.

Each book in this series explores the life of an endangered animal. The books tell how and why the animals have become endangered and explain the efforts being made to restore their populations.

The United States Fish and Wildlife Service and the National Marine Fisheries Service share responsibility for administration of the Endangered Species Act. Over time, animals are added to, reclassified in, or removed from the federal list of Endangered and Threatened Wildlife and Plants. At the time of publication, all the animals in this series were listed as endangered species. The most up-to-date list can be found at **http://www.fws.gov/endangered/wildlife.html**.

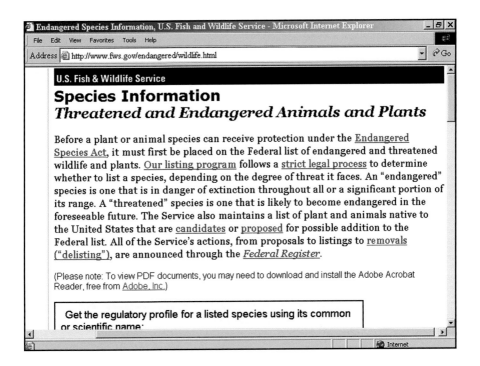

Report Links

The Internet sites described below can be accessed at
http://www.myreportlinks.com

▶**Crocodylus acutus**
Editor's Choice A Web site on the American crocodile includes maps, photos, and conservation plans.

▶**Animal Diversity Web: Crocodylus acutus**
Editor's Choice A university Web site offers a fact sheet on the American crocodile.

▶**Crocodiles!**
Editor's Choice This PBS site features fascinating photos of crocodiles.

▶**Endangered!: American Crocodile**
Editor's Choice Visit the American Museum of Natural History's site on the American crocodile.

▶**The American Crocodile: A Story of Recovery**
Editor's Choice "Croc Docs" tells the story of the American crocodile's recovery in Florida.

▶**Crocodile Specialist Group**
Editor's Choice Visit the site of an international network dedicated to saving the world's crocodiles.

▶**Alligators vs Crocodiles**
Learn how to tell the differences between alligators and crocodiles.

▶**American Crocodile**
A digital library of endangered species images is offered by this unique site.

▶**American Crocodile Crocodylus acutus**
A university's brief account of the American crocodile is offered by this site.

▶**Animal Ambassadors**
A government science center introduces crocs and alligators to Florida's human population.

▶**AquaFacts: Crocodilians**
An aquarium Web site answers questions about crocs.

▶**CITES Identification Guide—Crocodilians**
The CITES Identification Guide to Crocodilians is provided on this Web site.

▶**"Conservationists Prowl Swamps to Save Florida Crocs"**
Read about conservationists who trudge through Florida's swamps to save crocodiles.

▶**Crocodile Conservation Program**
The efforts of the Wildlife Conservation Society to save crocodilians is examined.

▶**Crocodile Photo Gallery**
A photo gallery of crocodiles is offered by this site.

MyReportLinks.com Books

Report Links

The Internet sites described below can be accessed at
http://www.myreportlinks.com

▶**The Crocodile's Power Play**
Read about one of the American crocodile's most unusual nesting sites.

▶**Endangered Species: Everglades National Park**
Learn about the endangered species that can be found in Everglades National Park.

▶**Everglades National Park**
Visit Everglades National Park, where the American crocodile and American alligator coexist.

▶**Ferocious Crocs**
This *Animal Planet* Web site takes visitors on a "tour" of a crocodile's body and more.

▶***National Geographic:* American Crocodile**
View this *National Geographic* profile of the American crocodile.

▶**Promise for the Survival of the Orinoco Crocodile**
Conservation efforts for the rare Orinoco crocodile are examined.

▶**Reptiles: Alligator and Crocodile**
A zoo Web site offers a fact-filled page on alligators and crocodiles.

▶**Reptile Trade: Crocodiles and Alligators**
Threats to crocodiles in the form of poachers are examined in this site.

▶**SuperCroc: *Sarcosuchus imperator***
Enter the Science of SuperCroc exhibit to investigate the world of an ancient crocodilian.

▶**U.S. Fish and Wildlife Service: Coastal Program**
What is a coastal ecosystem? This Fish and Wildlife Service site answers that question.

▶**U.S. Fish and Wildlife Service Species Profile: American Crocodile**
Read regulatory documents about Fish and Wildlife's plan to save the American crocodile.

▶**USFWS Endangered Species Program Kid's Corner**
This USFWS Web site offers ways you can help save endangered species.

▶**When Crocodiles Ruled**
A natural-history museum profiles the ancestors of crocodilians.

▶**World of the Crocodilians**
An interactive map helps readers see the worldwide habitats of crocodilians.

▶**Write Your Representative**
Find links to your congressional representatives on this government site.

baseline data—Initial scientific information collected at one particular time in order to establish a starting point and comparison point for future studies.

biodiversity—Describes an ecosystem in which there are a number of different species of animals and plants. Ecosystems that support more plants and animals are healthier than those in which only a few species can or do live.

captive breeding—Removing individual animals of an endangered species from the wild, breeding them in zoos, and returning their offspring to the wild.

carnivore—A meat-eating animal.

carrion—The dead carcass of an animal eaten by another animal.

clutch—The total group of eggs found in a nest.

critical habitat—Under the Endangered Species Act, the entire functioning ecosystem in which an endangered animal lives.

degradation (of habitat)—Damage done to habitat by human intervention in which an ecosystem's ability to support life is diminished.

ecosystem—All the resources, habitats, and plants and animals of a natural area that exist in a complex relationship, depending upon each other for survival.

ecotourism—Vacations that focus on wildlife and the natural places in which animals live, while being careful not to harm the animals or their habitat.

encroachment—An advance beyond the limits of one's territory.

estuary—A partially enclosed coastal body of water where seawater and freshwater mix.

exotic species—Also called invasive species, these are species of plants and animals that are introduced into a region and which then take over from, and drive out, native species.

incubation—The period between the laying of an egg and its hatching.

infrasound—Low frequency body vibrations used by crocodilians as a means of communication

insectivore—An insect-eating animal.

mangrove—A tropical tree that sends out many roots and forms dense masses. Mangroves are important to tropical ecosystems because they allow for coastal land building and are the foundation of unique ecosystems.

paleontologist—A scientist who studies fossil remains.

poaching—Illegal hunting for an animal or plant.

poikilothermic—Describes an animal whose internal temperature varies depending on external air and water temperatures.

polygynous—Describes a male that may mate with several females.

predation—The killing of animals as prey for food.

reptile—A cold-blooded, egg-laying, air-breathing animal with a backbone.

salinity—The amount of salt in a substance, such as a body of water.

scutes—Bony plates or scales like those found on a crocodilian.

sexual maturity—The age at which an animal can first mate.

sustainability—The ability of an ecosystem to remain healthy and support the life within it.

tsunami—A great sea wave produced by movement under the sea or a volcanic eruption.

Chapter 1. Meeting With a Crocodile

1. Dr. Frank J. Mazzotti, Associate Professor, University of Florida, Fort Lauderdale Research and Education Center, personal interview, March 7, 2006.

2. Ibid.

3. Ibid.

4. Ibid.

5. Ibid.

6. Ibid.

7. Ibid.

8. Department of the Interior, U.S. Fish and Wildlife Service, "Endangered and Threatened Wildlife and Plants; Reclassifying the American Crocodile Distinct Population Segment in Florida From Endangered to Threatened and Initiation of a 5-Year Review," *Federal Register*, March 25, 2005, vol. 70, no. 56, p. 15052.

9. Mazzotti interview.

10. Ibid.

11. Ibid.

12. Ibid.

13. Ibid.

Chapter 2. All About the American Crocodile

1. Charles A. Ross, ed., *Crocodiles and Alligators* (New York: Facts On File, Inc., 1989), p. 14.

2. Crocodile Specialist Group, Florida Museum of Natural History, University of Florida, Gainesville, *Crocodilians Natural History & Conservation*, "*Crocodylus acutus*" n.d., <http://www .flmnh.ufl.edu/cnhc/csp_cacu.htm> (November 28, 2006).

3. John and Deborah Behler, *Alligators & Crocodiles* (Stillwater, Minn.: Voyageur Press, 1998), p. 20.

4. Ross, p. 83.

5. Ibid., p. 106.

6. Ibid.

7. Ibid., p. 104

8. Ibid., p. 107.

9. Ibid., p. 150.

10. Environmental Protection Agency/Queensland Parks and Wildlife Service, "Mangroves," October 11, 2005, <http://www.epa.qld.gov.au/nature_conservation/habitats/wetlands/wetlands_habitats/mangroves/> (November 28, 2006).

11. James Perran Ross, ed., IUCN/SSC Crocodile Specialist Group, *Crocodile Status Survey and Conservation Action Plan, 2nd ed.,* 1998, Florida Museum of Natural History, University of Florida, Gainesville, <http://www.flmnh.ufl.edu/natsci/herpetology/act-plan/cacut.htm#J2> (November 28, 2006).

12. Jeff Klinkenberg, "Real Florida: The Long and Short of Crocodile Tales," *St. Petersburg Times,* September 5, 2002, <http://www.sptimes.com/2002/09/05/Floridian/Real_Florida__The_lon.shtml> (November 28, 2006).

13. Dr. Frank J. Mazzotti, personal interview, March 7, 2006.

Chapter 3. Threats to the Species

1. State of Florida, "Habitat Loss," *Florida Panther Net,* n.d., <http://www.panther.state.fl.us/handbook/threats/loss.html> (November 28, 2006).

2. South Florida Multi-Species Recovery Plan, 1999, "American Crocodile," p. 512.

3. Curtis Morgan, "Rising Sea Is Future Threat," *MiamiHerald.com,* May 29, 2006, <http://www.miami.com/mld/miamiherald/news/14692601.htm > (November 28, 2006).

4. South Florida Multi-Species Recovery Plan, 1999, "American Crocodile," p. 513.

Chapter 4. Protecting the American Crocodile

1. *National Park Service, Everglades National Park,* Deborah Nordeen, "South Florida's Watery Wilderness Nears Fifty," January 6, 1999, <http://www.nps.gov/ever/eco/nordeen.htm (November 28, 2006).

2. Paul Moler, personal interview, March 7, 2006.

3. Florida Power & Light, "Providing a home for the American Crocodile: A fact sheet about American crocodiles at Turkey Point."

4. Paul Moler, personal interview, March 7, 2006.

5. John Caldwell, *United Nations Environment Programme—World Conservation Monitoring Centre,* International Alligator and Crocodile Trade Study, "World Trade in Crocodilian Skins, 1999–2001," May 2003.

Chapter 5. Current Status and Conservation Efforts

1. James Perran Ross, ed., IUCN/SSC Crocodile Specialist Group, *Crocodile Status Survey and Conservation Action Plan, 2nd ed.,* 1998, Florida Museum of Natural History, University of Florida, Gainesville, <http://www.flmnh.ufl.edu/natsci/herpetology/act-plan/cacut .htm#J2> (November 28, 2006).

Chapter 6. Chances for Survival and Recovery

1. Dr. Frank J. Mazzotti, personal interview, March 7, 2006.

2. Paul Moler, personal interview, March 7, 2006.

3. James Perran Ross, ed., IUCN/SSC Crocodile Specialist Group, *Crocodile Status Survey and Conservation Action Plan, 2nd ed.,* 1998, Florida Museum of Natural History, University of Florida, Gainesville, <http://www.flmnh.ufl.edu/natsci/herpetology/act-plan/cacut .htm#J2> (November 28, 2006).

4. Dr. Frank J. Mazzotti, personal interview, March 7, 2006.

5. Ibid.

Chapter 7. Science, Sanctuary, and Sustainability

1. Michelle P. Moller, Michael S. Cherkiss, and Frank J. Mazzotti, "American Crocodile, *Crocodylus acutus:* An Endangered Species Recovery in Progress," a brochure published by the University of Florida, Fort Lauderdale Research and Education Center, and the U.S. Fish and Wildlife Service, South Florida Office, 2004.

Friend, Sandra. *Florida.* Watertown, Mass.: Charlesbridge Publishing, 2004.

Grace, Catherine O'Neill. *I Want to Be an Environmentalist.* San Diego: Harcourt, 2000.

Marx, Trish. *Everglades Forever: Restoring America's Great Wetland.* New York: Lee and Low Books, 2004.

Miller, Ruth. *Animal Kingdom: Reptile.* Oxford: Raintree Publishers, 2004.

Mongillo, John, and Linda Zierdt-Warshaw. E*ncyclopedia of Environmental Science.* Phoenix: Oryx Press, 2000.

National Geographic Animal Encyclopedia. Washington, D.C.: National Geographic Society, 2000.

Snyder, Trish. *Alligator and Crocodile Rescue: Changing the Future for Endangered Wildlife.* Buffalo: Firefly Books Ltd., 2006.

Stewart, Melissa. *Life in a Wetland.* Minneapolis: Lerner Publications, 2003.

Thomas, Isabel. *Alligator vs. Crocodile.* Oxford: Raintree Publishers, 2006.

Twist, Clint. *Reptiles and Amphibians Dictionary: An A to Z of Cold-blooded Creatures.* San Diego: Blackbirch Press, 2005.